MEthinks

Thinks

Random Thoughts on Life's Wrinkles

Mary Ellen Edmunds

DESERET BOOK

Salt Lake City, Utah

To Leanne

Thank you for persistent encouragement

Library of Congress Cataloging-in-Publication Data

Edmunds, Mary Ellen, 1940-
  MEE thinks : random thoughts on life's wrinkles / Mary Ellen Edmunds.
    p. cm.
  ISBN 1-59038-312-5 (pbk.)
  1. Christian life—Mormon authors. I. Title: Mary Ellen Edmunds thinks.
II. Title.
  BX8656.E36 2004
  248.4'89332—dc22
                                    2004001491

Printed in the United States of America   54459-081P
Malloy Lithographing Incorporated, Ann Arbor, MI

10   9   8   7   6   5

Contents

Contents

Preface

I love to think. Lots of times when people ask me about my hobbies or interests, I'll include "thinking." This love might be an extension or continuation of the daydreaming I did so much when I was younger—those trips to "La-La Land" in my mind where I could go anywhere, be anyone, do anything. I know that imagination still has a lot to do with it. I'm sure my thinking isn't always so wonderful as to be considered important—like pondering, meditating, or contemplating—but I do enjoy it.

I've decided I'd like to share some of the things I've been thinking about and see what *you* think. What I'd really like is for you to think with me.

You'll notice that I've used my initials in the title of this book: *MEE.* I've used these initials my whole life, almost as a nickname. Kind of a double meaning there: "MEE Thinks." Each chapter—except they don't really feel like "chapters"—each thought will begin the same: "I've been thinking about . . ." and then, off we go.

You'll also notice that some of the thoughts in this book are rather short. Even so, I hope something I share will spark an idea in you and give you a good thinking experience. Maybe it will be a memory. Maybe it will even be a plan taking shape in your heart and mind of something you want to do. Enjoy the ride!

I'd like to thank the excellent team at Deseret Book for all the work and attention to detail it takes to produce a book. In particular I thank my editor, Emily Watts, who is a wonderful genius as well as a happifying friend. Thanks to all who worked on this project!

Oh—and because I love to think and learn, I want to make it possible for others to do the same. Part of the income from this book will go to the Perpetual Education Fund of The Church of Jesus Christ of Latter-day Saints. Thanks for helping!

The Parade of Homes

I've been thinking about the event called the Parade of Homes.

I'm not sure why that came into my mind, but one day when I was thinking I decided to pretend that my home was selected to be in the Parade of Homes. This annual event showcases the latest in architecture, floor plans, and home furnishings in our area. Wow! With its incredible collection of dust balls, the unfinished basement, the cluttered garage, the vacuum weighing twenty-seven pounds, and the many beautiful spiderwebs, my home was to be part of the parade!

I have a sign inside that says, "You can look at the dust, but please don't write in it!" And then someone gave me a plaque that says, "You can write in the dust, but please don't date it!"

What I learned from this line of thought came into my heart when I began writing a description of my home

1

for the brochure, the Parade of Homes program. Some instructions were whispered to me: "Don't start with things like 'Sorry about the sidewalk in back—it fell in when they dug up the yard to put in the sewer system.' "Don't write about how horrible the flood was." I knew I wasn't supposed to describe what didn't work or what I wished I could do that I had not yet done. No, I was instructed to describe the *home* part, not the *house* part. And that made all the difference.

I'm sure that by the time I finished writing the description in my mind, which description I was going to submit to the brochure committee, it was much longer and more detailed than was appropriate. But what a wonderful journey! I started with the huge sign out in front: "Missionary Training Center." I described how it got there twenty years or so ago, all 600 pounds of it (it has a cement base), and how I think it would look nice as a part of a headstone for me someday.

I told about "PK Pine" growing in the backyard, and how it came to be—a gift from dear friends after my daddy went Home. I told about my wonderful peach tree, which has only one little limb left because it's old and keeps falling apart when the snow is heavy or the wind too strong. There are still peaches every summer, and oh, they're sweet! I explained about the apple tree and how it was planted "leaning into the wind" to try to ensure that it would grow straight. (It still leans into the wind a bit.)

I described the place I call the "Grand Canyon," and showed how I can look out a little window facing south and almost feel like I'm somewhere in the Grand Canyon when it rains. I showed where some friends had tried to prepare a garden spot one summer, and how the rocks had been too plentiful for the kind of time, equipment, and energy available.

Eventually I went inside and began my description of a refuge . . . a safe place . . . a home that was dedicated by my dear father on Sunday, May 7, 1995. I went from room to room, describing and explaining, enjoying the feeling that I didn't have to "justify" the way things were organized or disorganized. My goal was to tell why I love this home so much and why it is "just right" for me. I had the chance to share what I've done and am still doing to invite the Spirit to come and be with me always, and the ways in which I've put reminders all over the home of the things that are most important in my life: my relationship with my Heavenly Father and the Savior, my family and friends, and all else that matters most.

As I said, this was just in my imagination, but it brought me a great sense of gratitude and peace to see my wonderful home in a new and meaningful way. My home will never be on any official Parade of Homes, but it is just exactly what I need and want at this time in my life. It is an important part of my wholeness, wellness, happiness, peace, gratitude, and contentment.

I'd like to invite you to do the same thing. I live alone, so I prepared my description alone, but if you live with others, consider including them if it's something they'd enjoy. See what you learn, alone and together, as you describe your home, apartment, condo—the place where you live. Maybe you could start with things like:

"Love is spoken here."

"We have chosen to serve the Lord."

"We're trying a little harder to be a little better."

"There are moments when it feels like Heaven, and we're working to make that happen more often."

You may find you'll begin thinking of things for the brochure that a lot of people may not understand:

"This is where we have family prayer."

"This is where the young adults gathered for firesides."

"This is the table where we play Chicken Foot."

What do you think?

Materialism

I've been thinking about materialism again.

One of the ways I avoid materialism is by letting some of my dreams be enough.

Cancer and the Devil

I've been thinking about cancer and the devil.

It happened when I was a student nurse in about 1960. I was attending Brigham Young University but living at the time in the nurses' residence at LDS Hospital, on the corner of 8th Avenue and "C" Street in Salt Lake City.

I had begun my rotation in surgery. It was time to watch my very first "grand opening." The patient was an older woman—she was in her forties. I was not yet twenty, so forty seemed old to me.

She had cancer, but the doctors weren't sure exactly where or how extensive it was. They were going to perform a laparotomy to try to determine what was going on and how they might help.

I scrubbed to get ready to go into the operating room. We used a scrub brush, and it seemed as if at least two layers of skin between my fingertips and elbows disappeared as I scrubbed hard for the required number of minutes.

Eventually I was covered in a green gown, with green booties over my shoes, a green cap over my head, and a white cloth mask covering my mouth and nose. Then came the trick of putting on my sterile rubber gloves. It really was a trick: We practiced and practiced putting them on without touching "unclean" to "sterile."

Into the operating room I went, keeping my hands "front and center." I could hear our instructor's voice telling us never to let our hands stray away from where we could see them (to make sure they didn't touch anything that wasn't sterile).

They brought the woman into the room on a gurney. I remember feeling something like panic. "They're going to hurt her! They're going to cut her!" I almost felt I had a responsibility to protect her.

But some other part of me realized that the surgeon and all who would assist him were trying to help her. They were trying to find out what was making her so sick so they could figure out what they needed to do next in their efforts to save her life.

I learned something powerful that day. I saw cancer for the first time, up close and personal. I hated it immediately. There was a discoloration of tissue where it had entwined itself in and around the organs in the body of that woman.

It seemed to me that the cancer was trying to sneak around, hiding behind and inside, not wanting to show any signs or symptoms until it would be too late.

That's when I began to see the analogy between cancer and the devil. I think the devil also tries to sneak around, hiding behind and inside, not wanting to let any signs or symptoms show until someone is far from the iron rod, far from the straight and narrow path where there is safety.

There are new, effective ways to detect cancer. There are machines, procedures, and tests that can help patients and physicians know much earlier than they could in 1960 that something extremely unhealthy is at work, destroying and ruining parts of a healthy body and system.

There are even more effective ways to detect evil in our lives. We have light inside of us, and a "still small voice," and we are warned at the instant we let go of the iron rod or put our feet just barely off of the straight, narrow, safe path.

How do you get reminded or warned? Is there

anything going on in your heart or your life that isn't showing outward symptoms yet, but you know something's happening? Is it time to call the "spiritual hot line" for help? If you wait for more symptoms, will it be too late? What do you think?

Balance

I've been thinking about balance.

For this one you're going to have to have an imagination. Picture in your mind one of those scales with little dishes on both sides. Isn't there one of those in some picture where there's a woman with a blindfold on and she's measuring out justice? That's one kind, but the one I've been thinking about is where you have a bunch of beans or something on one side and maybe weights on the other, and you try to make them balance.

Another image to describe what I've been thinking is that of a teeter-totter. It's been a while since I've found anyone who could enjoy that particular "sport" with me—I'd flip 'em up into the trees! I remember when my brother got me up in the air once and then walked away. There was that split second when I realized I was going to go boom . . . and then I did. Anyway, think of a teeter-totter, or one of the scales with the little scoops where you can weigh things.

10

Ready? Now, while you're picturing this balancing image, think about your life. On the one side, stack up all the things that tend to be frustrating and discouraging. That's right—stack 'em up high and deep. Everything. Imagine them as little blocks or bottles or rocks with words carved into them: *Impatience, Laundry, Exercise, Road Rage, The Garage.* Put experiences there too, heartaches and heartbreaks and disappointments, all your suffering, all the unkindness, and all that has seemed so unfair.

When you've finished stacking all those hard things up, put the Savior on the other side, and see how quickly and completely things even out and become balanced. We can't put enough on the one side to make it impossible for Him to lift our burdens. He invites us to seek, ask, and knock, and I've never at any time or place read that He said, "It isn't about ordinary things; only seek, ask, and knock about *big* things."

Do we shut Him out of our daily lives? Do we imagine that He wouldn't be interested in hearing about or helping with our daily routine? I love the phrase "reaches my reaching" (*Hymns,* no. 129), which illustrates for me the truth that He asks us to do the best we can and then to ask for His help with what we can't do. How in the world (interesting phrase, isn't it, *in the world*) can we ever get anywhere in any aspect of our lives without asking Him to help? I'm certainly not advocating that we make our list of things to do, tape it on the fridge, and ask Him to take over while we sit and read the latest political thriller or put a puzzle together or watch "soaps." Of course not. There's something wonderful about doing all we can do and then seeking His help to balance out the rest—not to do it for us, but in a way to do it *with* us, showing us better ways to manage our time and other resources.

It's been my experience that the Savior will never whisper something in our hearts like "That was so easy; I can't believe you couldn't do that!" Rather, I imagine Him saying, "Thanks for letting me help you. I knew you could do it!"

The Big Bad Wolf

I've been thinking about the Big Bad Wolf.

If I asked you to sing the "Big Bad Wolf" song with me, could you do it? Imagine in your mind a pig trio, and yourself singing with them, "Who's afraid of the Big Bad Wolf, the Big Bad Wolf, the Big Bad Wolf," and so on.

I'm afraid of the Big Bad Wolf! I admit it! I'm also afraid of, or at least made nervous by, spiders and snakes and several other things. What are your "wolves"? What are some things you're afraid of?

There actually are some interesting things we can learn about dealing with danger from the story of the Big Bad Wolf and the Three Little Pigs. The wolf seemed relentless in his pursuit of the little pigs. He kept thinking of ways to get them. He tried sneaking up on them as well as challenging them directly (the part about "I'll huff and I'll puff!"). And the piggies seemed to be pretty insecure—especially the ones who weren't surrounded by bricks. There was this constant danger that they were going to be eaten by the Big Bad Wolf. The straw and sticks that may have seemed adequate at first eventually were shown to be too flimsy.

The Savior taught about wolves who would try to disguise themselves in sheep's clothing in attempts to do harm to the flock. He also taught about ways to build shelters that wouldn't disappear in the storms to come. He talked about counting the cost first, about making sure our shelter would be built upon a rock rather than sand. He asked us not to be foolish. In some ways He might have been saying, "Choose bricks!" Actually, He was saying, "Choose Me! Establish your lives, your shelter, and your security in Me."

Christ can help us to recognize the Big Bad Wolf no matter *what* kind of disguise or trick that wolf may use to try to frighten and destroy us. What can you do today to build your home with His materials?

Ersatz

I've been thinking about *ersatz*.

I think my dad was the first person I heard use the word *ersatz,* but I first came to understand what it meant in November of 1965 when the real Maria Von Trapp came to speak at BYU. It was an incredible experience to actually meet her and listen to her after having so recently been captivated by Julie Andrews in *The Sound of Music.* She shared some of her memories of what life had been like after the First World War. One of her memories was of being a very hungry little girl:

"I was so hungry that it hurt—all the time. I remembered how nothing was left, and we got—and this is an untranslated word—we got 'ersatz' for every real thing. 'Ersatz' means a less good thing for the good one that isn't there. So we got some brown liquid, which was called 'ersatz' coffee. Or we got 'ersatz' material for the real one—something made of paper and we were warned not to go out with it in the rain. We got wooden shoes, 'ersatz' shoes. And so it was 'ersatz' all over, until Austria picked herself up again, and after a few years quietly the real thing came back and nobody talked about the 'ersatz' anymore" (Baroness Maria Von Trapp, November 18, 1965, *BYU Speeches of the Year,* 1965, 10).

Ersatz, then, is a substitute for the real thing. It's fake. My dad told me stories about when he was on his mission in Germany in the early 1920s, and what inflation did to that country following World War I. One way he illustrated was to tell me how he made a bill for thousands of marks, and a storekeeper actually took it when Dad went to buy bread. He immediately told the storekeeper that he had made it—that it was an ersatz bill—but the storekeeper shrugged and said it didn't matter. Normally the mark had stood at about 4 marks for $1.00. By January 1920, it was about 50 marks per $1.00. It went to 188 by January 1922 and had climbed to 7,650 by the end of 1922. One year later, in December 1923, it was 4,200,000,000,000 marks per $1.00! (see Trebor H. Tims, "'Vampire' Currency: A Million for a Loaf of Bread," *Improvement Era,* October 1933).

Those who make counterfeit money as a "profession" get pretty good, to the point where many are fooled, but the bills are never exactly the same as the real thing. No matter how good they get or how many are fooled, the bills are still ersatz money. On money and checks there are often symbols or designs that show up only when the paper is held up to the light. It's as if the light can help determine whether something is real or ersatz—genuine or a fake.

Here's my point: I don't want to be an imitation of a real friend or an ersatz Christian. I'm thinking of something the great prophet Nephi said as he finished his long and glorious mission among his people: "Wherefore, my beloved brethren, I know that if ye shall follow the Son, with full purpose of heart, acting no hypocrisy and no deception before God, but with real intent, repenting of your sins, witnessing unto the Father that ye are willing to take upon you the name of Christ, by baptism—yea, by following your Lord and your Savior down into the water, according to his word, behold, then shall ye receive the Holy Ghost; yea, then cometh the baptism of fire and of the Holy Ghost; and then can ye speak with the tongue of angels, and shout praises unto the Holy One of Israel" (2 Nephi 31:13).

I want to especially focus on the part about following the Son "with full purpose of heart, acting no hypocrisy and no deception before God, but with real intent." Thinking about these words and phrases makes me wonder if I'm sometimes "acting," that my devotion is ersatz . . . merely a substitute for the real thing, for true conversion, worship, and following. I have to smile, almost, when I think about "acting no hypocrisy and no deception before God." How could I ever even imagine that that would be possible? Acting before God, who knows my every thought and the desires of my heart? Imagine me trying to put any smidgeon of deception past Him! Imagine me trying to go before Him without real intent, but just to go through the motions. Ersatz. Imitation. Substitution. What would I expect in return for such pretense and hypocrisy?

I think of being held up to some light (the Light of the World?), and I would hope something real would show up—something indicating that through my efforts I had become a genuine follower of Christ. Oh, how I pray we may always follow the Son with full purpose of heart!

Fellowshipping

I've been thinking about fellowshipping.

One day when I was thinking about it, I had an imaginary scene come into my mind. There was a little ship out in the ocean in a terrible storm. It was tossing around, and as the waves and storm grew stronger, there was an increasing likelihood that the little ship was going to tip over and sink and be lost forever.

But then here came little fellow ships, venturing out in the storm, finding the ship that was in trouble, surrounding it, and safely guiding it to a protected harbor.

Can you think of someone who's being tossed around in a terrible storm who might be searching through the darkness for a fellow ship to come to the rescue?

Laughter

I've been thinking about laughter.

I think it's in the *Reader's Digest* that they call laughter "the best medicine." Have you had times when a good laugh did make you feel like you'd had a dose of needed medicine? Do you ever hear or see or read or experience something and wish you could laugh even harder than you do? I probably feel that way too often, but I can't really explain what I mean. I just know that I love to laugh.

One winter's morning during a snowstorm I took my mother to the lab for some blood tests. We had to drive about twenty-six miles round-trip, and it was "white-knuckle" driving for sure. We saw a bunch of "fender-benders"—accidents where no one was seriously injured but a whole lot of people had sure had their day ruined. We were headed home and going around a corner very slowly. I would estimate we were going about one mile an hour, if that. The car hit black ice, and slowly we headed for the curb and hit it with a "thunk"!

I asked Mom instantly, "Are you okay?" She said she was. I got the car away from the curb and we continued cautiously and slowly up the road. Then I said, in an oh-so-sarcastic kind of way, "So I suppose you're going to sue me for whiplash . . ." Instantly she jumped in with some moaning, holding her neck. "Oh . . . ohhhhhh . . . oh, my neck hurts . . . oh, I can't move my head . . . oh dear, I have to call . . ." and she tried to say the name of one of the lawyers who advertises on TV that you should contact them in the event of an accident. It was so spontaneous and so hilarious that we both laughed until we were screaming unbecomingly. We eventually came up for air, but Mom kept the fun going for several days, calling me the next morning and moaning and whining about her whiplash the minute I answered.

I have heard that if you want to laugh or need to laugh and you don't—when you suppress laughter—it goes to your hips and spreads out. How can I find out if this is true or not? It sounds possible and dangerous!

Often, laughter is the shortest distance between two people, including two people who don't have a common spoken language. And it can be like a needed break, a tiny vacation, even. It can be comforting. I was so touched when, a few weeks after our dad went Home, my sister Charlotte put some of her favorite cartoons, saved over many years, in an envelope and handed it to me to help cheer me up as I was leaving on a speaking trip. I sat in the airport laughing, and it felt so good.

I laughed when I first heard about neighbors organizing to have a "Cul-de-Sac of Fire" when they couldn't make it to a "Stadium of Fire" Fourth of July celebration. My friend Helen told me of some people in Vernon, Utah, who, faced with way too many crickets in 1999, included in their ward newsletter some cricket recipes! Terrific!

I have a special admiration for those who can laugh through their troubles. Try this sometime when you're having a not-so-good day. When someone says, "Good morning," respond with, "Well, you got it half right . . ." Picture the person thinking about that for the rest of the day and maybe being helped to smile out loud.

President Ezra Taft Benson said: "One great thing the Lord requires of each of us is to provide a home where a happy, positive influence for good exists. In future years the costliness of home furnishings or the number of bathrooms will not matter much, but what will matter significantly is whether our children felt love and acceptance in the home. It will greatly matter whether there was happiness and laughter, or bickering and contention" (*Ensign,* May 1981, 34).

I grew up in a home where there was happiness and laughter (along with probably too much bickering and contention; we had opposition in all things). We now just have to give the "punch lines" to get the laughter started at jokes and experiences that go way, way back. Try saying "It's either a skunk or a weasel!" to someone in my family and see what happens!

Lighten your day by thinking about your own "family funnies." This will really lift your spirits. Think with MEE! Laugh with MEE!

Moving Walkways

I've been thinking about moving walkways.

You know the drill: "The moving walkways are for your convenience. Please stand to the right in single file, allowing others to pass you on the left. Thank you for your courtesy."

So imagine this: You're in a *huge* airport, you're in a *hurry,* your bags are *so heavy* [quit crying; I know this is bringing specific moments back to you, but hang in there], it's five *miles* to the gate for your connecting flight . . . and then you see it: the moving walkway! You're not walking any faster, but your walking is enhanced.

I think about life. I think of how hard it can be in some moments or seasons to get from where we are to where we need to be. Heavenly Father really can and does help us get where we're going, even when we have heavy, heavy burdens. He can stretch our walking, our minutes, our pennies, our hearts, and anything else that needs stretching! He reaches our reaching and stretches our stretching. His "moving walkways" are everywhere. You watch. You'll see them. You've probably already used them many, many times.

Observing

I've been thinking about observing.

I've lived in Mapleton, Utah, since 1957. I know some of you will be so surprised that I was even born by 1957. Ha ha ha. In the many years that I've lived in Mapleton, I've driven to and from famous places literally hundreds of times. For example, I've driven to and from the Missionary Training Center in Provo for years—back and forth, back and forth. And to and from the Springville Post Office tons of times! And to and from BYU so many times I can't even count them. And yet . . . and yet there will be a moment when I see something I've never seen before. It's been there all the time. A little home. A tree. A garden or a bush. A sign. A rock. A boy on a bicycle . . . (okay, I can tell I'm beginning to descend into silliness, so I'll move on).

This is what I've begun to learn from realizing how unaware and unobservant I can be and have been: What is it I fail to notice in people, and in my relationships with my Heavenly Father, the Savior, and the Holy Ghost? How much richer and fuller (and more interesting!) could and will my life be if I notice what's around and inside of me?

This ties in to the thinking I've been doing about sight and insight. Think of all you can see with your natural eyes. And in case someone is reading this to you and you can't see with your natural or physical eyes, think of all the ways in which other aspects of your perception have been heightened and purified.

If you do have the use of your eyes, think of the difference it makes when you use your glasses (and don't poke fun at us if you don't yet need them). Think of how words or other objects come into focus. Now think of a little magnifying glass, perhaps like one you used in elementary school. Did you ever catch the sun through it and start a little fire? (Don't try this at home!) It's as if you can see things that you wouldn't be able to see without help.

How about a big magnifying glass? I'm thinking of one my dad used to use when he'd work on crossword puzzles. It even had a light on it—magnification plus light was a wonderful thing! I love those dictionaries into which so much information is packed that you need a pretty good-sized magnifying glass to discover the "buried treasures" inside.

Think of binoculars. Have you ever used them at a sporting event or some other kind of performance? Binoculars bring things a lot closer, don't they? I'm even thinking of those 3-D movies I went to when I was much younger, where we'd put on the cardboard glasses with red on one side and green on the other that made it seem like the Three Stooges were throwing things (including each other) right in our faces! Think of microscopes and telescopes and planetariums and all the other ways in which our ability to see and perceive is enhanced and magnified.

If you're thinking with me, you've likely jumped ahead and will already know what I've been learning through pondering this stuff about awareness, observing, noticing, and perceiving. Think of times when God actually dropped the (physical) scales from someone's eyes and they could really see! I love hymn no. 143, "Let the Holy Spirit Guide." There's the wonderful phrase in the first verse, "Light our minds with heaven's view." Oh, the things we can see through the power and help of the Holy Spirit! I'd like to go through my days and experiences with more awareness of all that's around me and inside of me!

Security Checks

I've been thinking about security checks.

You know how you have to walk through a metal detector at the airport, to prove that you're not carrying any weapons or anything you're not supposed to have on a plane. These security checks seem much more thorough since the tragic events of September 11, 2001. I've even set off the alarm with a paper clip, and with the foil wrapper on my gum!

What if there were some kind of a "Charity Checkpoint" as you were trying to get to Heaven, kind of like these security checkpoints at airports, and if it detected any "alloys"—any inappropriate, "non-YOU" stuff—an alarm sounded. We would need to be *pure* to go through this Charity Checkpoint, so we need the deep waters and fiery trials of our lives so that all the dross—the impurities—can be removed. We need to deny ourselves of all ungodliness so that we are pure.

Maybe as we approach the Charity Checkpoint,

rather than asking, "Do you have a laptop?" someone will ask, "Do you have a lap? A used one? One that has held little children to soothe and comfort them, to read to them and teach them?" Perhaps we are given a chance to take everything out of our pockets and our hearts and our lives before we get to the final step. Maybe time is given to us to prepare to meet God.

Think what it would mean to be able to go through the Charity Checkpoint without sounding all kinds of alarms—"This one isn't filled with charity!" It shall be well with us (see Moroni 7) if we are filled with charity, if there's no envy left, no impatience, no unforgiveness, no unkind thoughts or evil desires. Walking back to our Heavenly Father, passing the angels who are on guard— what would that be like?

Thoughts

I've been thinking about thoughts.

I love to think. President Boyd K. Packer said that "thoughts are talks we hold with ourselves" (*Ensign,* November 1999, 24). I don't think I do enough of this—of talking to myself, pondering, really thinking carefully and considering deeply.

One day an idea came into my mind that has had a powerful effect on my understanding of why thinking and thoughts are so important. I imagined that someday, somewhere, Jesus may simply ask, "What's on your mind?" Wow! That may be a question I can ask myself often: "What's on your mind?"

This makes it a lot easier to understand why it's important to follow the counsel given in Doctrine and Covenants 121:45: "Let virtue [good, uplifting, edifying things] garnish thy thoughts unceasingly." I've considered what *garnish* means, feeling it probably meant the parsley on the plate of food in a restaurant—a decoration. Do we decorate our thoughts with virtue? I went to a big dictionary and found some good stuff. To garnish is to make beautiful! Then I found this definition: "To adorn with a commendable or excellent quality." Of course! We adorn our thoughts with that which is beautiful, commendable, and of excellent quality.

From our thoughts come our actions and our character, the words we say to each other, and the way we behave. And then there's the part about "unceasingly." That doesn't sound like an exercise for a few minutes a day, or just on the Sabbath. Unceasingly. Good thoughts constantly.

I was pretending once that the language of Heaven is not one where we're trying to reduce thoughts to words (trying to speak all languages to all people), but the ability to transmit our thoughts to each other, to "read" each other's thoughts! And I thought to myself that if that were true, no wonder we're to let virtue garnish our thoughts unceasingly! Everyone would be able to perceive what we were thinking!

I remember watching a TV show called *Magnum P.I.* in which the main character, played by Tom Selleck, would "think out loud," and many times would start a conversation with "I know what you're thinking." Likely there are times when we're pretty sure we know what someone else is thinking, or at least we can come close. How and why? Because of their actions and because of their words. We've probably all heard the saying, "Your actions speak so loudly that I can't hear what you're saying." Something like that. I also remember a song with words something like, "Your lips tell me 'no, no,' but there's 'yes, yes' in your eyes."

Well, every action and every word is preceded by thoughts, by thinking. As we let virtue garnish our thoughts unceasingly, how could hurtful, thoughtless, evil words and actions come from us? Am I sounding too simplistic? What do you think? Perhaps it's like Jesus teaching us that "by their fruits ye shall know them," and fruits come because seeds are planted. Remember how Alma invited the poor among the Zoramites to plant words in their hearts? (See Alma 32.) Good words—good thoughts—planted in our hearts bring forth good words spoken to others, and good actions. This may even tie into the law of the harvest. We reap what we sow. (When I was in 4-H it was "I rip what I sew.")

President Gordon B. Hinckley has reminded us of a significant promise attached to good thoughts: "The Lord has given a commandment in our time that applies to each of us. He has said, 'Let virtue garnish thy thoughts unceasingly.' And with this He has given a promise, 'then shall thy confidence wax strong in the presence of God' (D&C 121:45). I believe He is saying that if we are clean in mind and body, the time will come when we can stand confidently before the Lord just as Joseph F. Smith stood before the Prophet Joseph and said, 'I am clean.' There will be a feeling of confidence and there will also be smiles of approval" (*Ensign,* May 1996, 48).

Think of that. He goes on to say the Holy Ghost shall be our constant companion. Our dominion shall be an everlasting dominion (see D&C 121:45–46). What marvelous and remarkable promises these are, and they are given to those who walk in virtue.

We do become what we think about, what we allow to come into our minds and stay. And we really do eventually receive the true desires of our hearts. I am convinced that as we conquer our thoughts, we also can conquer and discipline and guide our actions, our words, and our lives. And then when Jesus asks, "What's on your mind?" we can share openly, honestly, with no hesitation.

Yard Sales

I've been thinking about yard sales.

That's a lot to sell—your yard. Some people sell their garages. I've been thinking about trying something a little different. See what you think. What if we skipped this "middle man" and took those same things to give away where they were needed? So keep your yard, and keep your garage, and clean out some closets and drawers and take things to Deseret Industries or Goodwill or next door or wherever they might be needed.

Pennies

I've been thinking about pennies.

I've heard there's a movement afoot to get rid of pennies. A clue on the TV show *Jeopardy* one day suggested that the zinc industry was becoming nervous because pennies might go away (and as if there weren't many other reasons I'll never be on *Jeopardy,* not knowing that pennies are mostly made of zinc is one reason).

I have mixed feelings about this. I kind of like pennies. I've always been one to pick up pennies. It's always been a "thing" between me and my dad. We'd say, when we saw one, "We still pick up pennies."

Another memory that concerns pennies was when my sister Charlotte was trying to learn about tithing. Mom would sit with her in the library, with the door closed, and the drill would begin. "You have ten pennies. How many pennies do you give to the Lord?" There was always a long pause, and then a meek little voice taking a guess. "Three?"

"No! No!" And Mom would remind her it was one penny. One. Then there was the day when I was once again listening on the other side of the door. Charlotte got it wrong again. "You have ten pennies. [Lots of emphasis]: How many pennies do you give to the Lord?"

The long pause. A humble "two?"

"No! No!"

And then Charlotte started to cry. "He can have them all! I don't want any pennies! Give them all to the Lord!"

In 1993, Mom had a stroke. One thing that happened was that numbers and words got all mixed up inside her brain. Gradually she learned to speak again, but she couldn't write, and she had trouble with numbers. It was a pretty funny day when Charlotte came to her and said, "You have ten pennies . . ."

Some of my favorite thoughts include pennies. "We may forget to thank Heavenly Father for five pennies if we're always whining for ten." Or, "A penny for your thoughts." A penny is a little thing for sure, but they can gather together and accomplish mighty things.

Manna

I've been thinking about manna.

The children of Israel were blessed with this daily food, and they were allowed to gather what they needed, "every man according to his eating" (Exodus 16:16). Apparently there was enough available for everyone, both those who ate little and those who ate a lot. No worries about what to fix, or where to find sticks to make a fire, or who would do the dishes after the meal.

Actually, I've been thinking about myself and manna. Sometimes I try to imagine how I would respond in some circumstance where I know something about how others have responded. So I imagine I'm out in the wilderness with the rest of the children of Israel, and we have manna for our food. At first I would have been so grateful to have something, anything, to eat. "Oh, thank you, thank you, thank you." I'd have said that to the one who brought the manna around to our camp. But I know myself. Pretty soon I'd have begun to murmur. "How come I can't have it *my* way?" "How do I super-size this?" "Where's your list of drinks?" "Why doesn't manna come in 31 flavors?" "Where's the dessert menu?" "This is a little chewy—do you have anything softer?"

I once heard someone say that all we'd ever want is a little more than we'd ever have. And as I've been thinking, an interesting thought has crept in. Let's suppose I was back there in the wilderness with manna. Let's suppose I was a wise little person and I was thankful for the manna. Is there just a chance that my manna would taste sweet and wonderful to me simply because I was so thankful and happy to have it? And imagine manna with quail! This was bread from heaven, never burned or "day-old" or anything like that! Fresh manna every single day, including the Sabbath, because we got to save some from our Saturday supply. That makes me think that maybe the little children back then sang a song something like, "Saturday is a special day, for we get to collect extra manna . . ."

Okay, that's just a little "demo" about the way I think—how I get all off the track because my imagination is such a lively thing. I was born with a BB condition: Busy Brain. So I'll get back to manna by sharing something wonderful that Elder Marion D. Hanks taught as he was speaking at Brigham Young University on March 25, 1980: "Gather the manna daily. Do you remember the great lesson the Lord taught the children of Israel in providing manna for them which they had to gather daily? They had been slaves in Egypt and had forgotten their relationship with the Lord. To teach them and prove them, the Lord required that they gather the manna every day except over the Sabbath. They could not collect it or store it. It had to be gathered every day. (See Ex. 16.) Spirituality, that condition of closeness with the Lord through his Spirit, is like manna to us. We cannot live well without it, and it must be gathered every day. It isn't enough to have known, to have read, to have given, to have prayed, to have obeyed. That great series of verses in Alma 5 that move me so much begins with, 'If ye have felt to sing the song of redeeming love, I would ask, can ye feel so now?' (See Alma 5:26–31.)" (*Ensign,* July 1981, 71–72).

There *is* a kind of manna for us to collect every day. It's the manna without which we cannot live: it's spirituality and closeness to the Savior. He declared, "I am the living bread which came down from heaven: if any man eat of this bread, he shall live for ever" (John 6:51). Once this thought comes into my heart, I'm really thinking. I'm going back to my "manna whining," wondering if I complain that I want gospel principles to be a "different flavor," or that things I read in the scriptures seem like "day-old" stuff. I also wonder whether there is any kind of mechanism inside of me that can give a "hungry" signal for that which is spiritual the way my stomach does when I'm hungry for physical food.

Am I ever like those who followed the Savior around hoping for loaves and fishes, not realizing what He really could give me, which would last forever? Listen to the way Elder Jeffrey R. Holland teaches this: "In that little story is something of the danger in our day. It is that in our contemporary success and sophistication we too may walk away from the vitally crucial bread of eternal life; we may actually *choose* to be spiritually malnourished, willfully indulging in a kind of spiritual anorexia. Like those childish Galileans of old, we may turn up our noses when divine sustenance is placed before us. Of course the tragedy then as now is that one day, as the Lord Himself has said, 'In an hour when ye think not the summer shall be past, and the harvest ended,' and we will find that our 'souls [are] not saved'" (*Ensign,* November 1997, 65).

I want to arise every day and experience a hunger for

my spiritual nourishment at least as strong as my desire for physical food. Maybe stronger. As much as I love bread, and I really do, I know I can't *live* with just bread. I need the sweet nourishment of the Spirit, the guidance and companionship of the Holy Ghost. And I have a feeling that an increase in my gratitude for this spiritual manna will bring an increase in the "nutrients" I find in my searching the scriptures, my praying, my renewing of covenants, my response to all that is available to me.

Noah's Ark

I've been thinking about Noah's ark.

I'm glad it was an ark rather than a boat or a ship. It just sounds better: Noah's ark.

While serving as a health missionary in the Philippines, I loved using a quote I'm sure you've heard before: "It wasn't raining when Noah built the ark." Kind of a fun way to teach preparedness and prevention. I was sent over to Hong Kong for a while, and we got that great quote translated into Chinese and had someone put the characters on a poster for us. Didn't work. The people would look at it, but no lights would come on. Oops! I still like the thought, though.

One reason I've thought a lot about this is because I wonder what things were like in his world as Noah was building that ark. Did everyone think he was nuts? Here was a man about 600 years old using all the gopher wood for miles around to build a huge vessel in the dry season.

Were there any who sincerely asked him what was going on, catching on that this was a prophet? Apparently not, because when it was time to get on board, it was just Noah, his wife, his sons and their wives, and a whole bunch of animals.

What about MEE? What about us? It's so easy to think we would have jumped in to help; we would never have snickered or even listened to the jokes about Noah. We would have stuck up for him.

How do I respond if the jokes are directed at me—if I'm trying to do what is right, and someone is poking fun, and I shrink a bit, slipping in my resolve. Elder Jeffrey R. Holland has said: "If you are trying hard and living right and things still seem burdensome and difficult, take heart. Others have walked that way before you. Do you feel unpopular and different or outside the inside of things? Read Noah again. Go out there and take a few whacks on the side of your ark and see what popularity was like in 2,500 B.C." (*New Era,* October 1980, 10).

Elder Neal A. Maxwell has a wonderful way of putting thoughts into words: "It has been asked, and well it might be, how many of us would have jeered, or at least been privately amused, by the sight of Noah building his ark. Presumably, the laughter and the heedlessness continued until it began to rain—and kept raining. How wet some people must have been before Noah's ark suddenly seemed the only sane act in an insane, bewildering situation!" (*New Era,* January 1971, 9).

I think of those who were left behind. What was it like when it started to rain? By the time outward circumstances had begun to convince people in the village that Noah had been right, the ark was shut. Hearts had not changed with truth, and once their outward circumstances changed their minds and convinced them Noah had been right, it was too late. One of my friends once said that "hell is truth seen too late." Wow.

What do *you* think? Were there people scratching and knocking and hollering as the waters and the ark rose? Were they trying to get Noah to listen to their outstanding reasons for needing to get on board?

Now bring those thoughts up to today. What are the indications (are there any?) that I am currently listening, paying attention, and following? I think of President Gordon B. Hinckley pleading with us to get out of debt. Have I done that? What have I been taught? Are there important truths in my life now that I've ignored or followed with only a portion of enthusiasm and a small part of my heart? How well do I listen to the Noahs of my day? How well have I followed that which latter-day prophets have asked me to do?

Elder Glenn L. Pace has expressed it so well: "Why do we sometimes find it easier to accept and follow past prophets? It is partly because history has proven their counsel to be sound. Future generations will find the same to be true of the prophets of our day" (*Ensign,* May 1989, 27).

What kinds of things will be asked of me—of us—as the time gets closer for the Savior to return? Will we be found mocking and ignoring? "But of that day, and hour, no one knoweth; no, not the angels of God in heaven, but my Father only. But as it was in the days of Noah, so it shall be also at the coming of the Son of Man" (Joseph Smith–Matthew 1:40–41).

This is our day to make choices, to be obedient, to repent, to follow a prophet. There is an ark for us, a place of safety and refuge in the midst of the floods of wickedness and temptation that surround us. The path to get on board is straight and narrow, with enough light and truth to show us the way.

Global Warming

I've been thinking about global warming.

This is a great concern to many people—global warming. One night I had an idea. It was one of those life-changing, world-changing ideas that arrive when you're not actually conscious. You write the idea down, positive it's a winner. Then, when you look at it later, you have no idea where it came from.

So here we go: my idea for dealing with global warming. I'm not sure it would work, but of course I'll share it anyway. I thought it might help if I planted a whole bunch of ice cubes, with the hope that they'd grow into glaciers and help the world cool down.

Language

I've been thinking about language.

I know a few words and phrases in a few languages, and I've come to realize that there are many lessons in the meanings of words. Think with MEE about the Indonesian language for a few minutes. Are you feeling adventurous? Are you willing to experiment a bit?

The Indonesian language—Bahasa Indonesia—is similar in its pronunciation rules to Spanish and other languages where the vowels have the same sound in every instance. *A* is *ah,* like in *law* and *ha* and *awe. E* is *eh,* like in *yet* and *set* and *met. I* is *ee,* like in *see* and *be* and *MEE. O* is *oh,* like in *show* and *flow* and *row. U* is *oo,* like in *you* and *flew* and *grew.* Have you got it? Let's try a few words.

First I want to assure you that you already know some Indonesian words. Would you like to know what they are? The first word is the one for *person.* It's *orang.* It almost sounds like "oh wrong." And the *r* is rolled a bit.

Don't worry if you can't do that part. The next word is *hutan,* pronounced kind of like "who tawn" (rhymes with *brawn*). This is the word for *jungle.* Sometimes it seems like the *h* is pronounced with a bit of a growl. Not any deep kind of growl, but just a little growl. Oh, never mind. Don't worry about that. *Person* is *orang,* and *jungle* is *hutan.* Put them together. *Orang hutan.* Say it out loud a couple of times. *Orang hutan, orang hutan.* Is it sounding at all familiar? What's the animal in the jungle that's sort of apelike and has a cute face? Right! Orangutan! Now whenever you see one of those cute apes you'll think, "Person of the jungle!" (And we're not talking Tarzan this time.)

Ready for more? How about this one: The word for *eye* is *mata* (rhymes with *oughta* or *gotta*). The word for *day* is *hari* (rhymes with *sorry*). *Mata hari. Eye day.* The eye of the day is the sun! The way to say *sun* in the Indonesian language is *mata hari!* These words may remind you of a famous spy, but she is no longer living, so I'll just stick with sun.

One thing that's fun to learn is how to ask the familiar, "How are you?" The way you do that in Indonesian is by asking, "Apa kabar?" *Apa* rhymes with *papa,* and *kabar* rhymes with nothing I can think of. Oh well. Do your best. *Apa* is *what,* and *kabar* is *news.* So you're asking "What news?" And the response? "Kabar baik" (sounds like *bike,* but I still don't know anything that rhymes with *kabar*). "News is good."

Are you bored? Please don't be bored. We're going to get to something important pretty soon here. Let's talk about saying "Good morning." The phrase is "Selamat Pagi." *Selamat* means *peace,* and *pagi* (the *g* is hard; kind of rhymes with *soggy*) means *morning.* So when you say to someone, "Selamat pagi," you're wishing them peace in the morning, a peaceful morning. And there's one word that is just plain great to have in your vocabulary (and then I promise I'll get closer to what we can think about). It's *bagus.* "Bah-goose." *Bagus* means wonderful, terrific, great, and so on.

Now to a fun word. The word for *teeth* is *gigi* (rhymes with *tee hee* with hard *g*'s). Isn't that fun to say? Then there's a word for someone who is not professional or highly educated. The word is *tukang.* You kind of "swallow" that *g.* *Tukang* sort of rhymes with *too gong.* So a *Tukang Gigi* would be someone who works on teeth without a lot of education or training (kind of scary, huh). An expert—someone with extensive education and training—is a *Juru.* That rhymes with *Guru* (another

Indonesian word, which means *teacher* or *mentor*). So a *Juru* is a professional. A *Juru Gigi* would be a dentist, for example. A *Juru* is an expert.

Now let's go back to the word for *peace*. Do you remember that? *Selamat*. Put that with the word for expert: *Juru. Juru Selamat.* Expert of Peace. These are the words for Jesus Christ—*Juru Selamat,* an Expert of Peace. I love it. He *is* an expert of peace. And we can do our best to be experts of peace as well—peacemakers. Think about ways you can continue doing that in quiet, wonderful ways. Blessed are the peacemakers. . . .

Elevators

I've been thinking about elevators, Otis and the others.

A few years ago I thought it would be fun to write a little book called "Between Floors," and it would be about elevators, specifically about talking on elevators. I wanted the book to give people a bit of a lift (ha ha ha). I even thought I might dedicate the book to my friend Ned Winder, because he made talking on elevators look so easy. The book didn't happen, but the thinking has continued.

I'm at the point where it's hard for me not to laugh right out loud when I'm getting on an elevator. People are chatting and sharing, but this ends (almost abruptly) when the doors open and we get inside the box. Everyone suddenly goes so quiet. We all seem to be reading about when Otis was last inspected, or what the capacity is. And we all face one direction—we face the doors. Here's a challenge for a day when you're feeling extra spunky: Get on last, and don't turn around . . . just face everyone. You can simply smile, or you can make funny faces, or you can say, "Hello, everyone" and see what reactions you get!

Sometimes I feel we're too isolated and insulated from each other. I know there are times when it's nice to be alone—to enjoy solitude—but do you ever wish you were better at making connections with other people? Do your memories sometimes take you back to junior high dances or birthday parties or other group activities where you felt painfully shy and awkward? Do some of those feelings continue to this day? Do you ever feel the desire to be a little or a lot more outgoing and friendly? Do you ever wish you had more courage in talking to people you don't know, or even sometimes to people you do know?

For a bunch of years (at least 25, but fewer than 200), I've had this "thing" about talking on elevators. I think it's one of the five or ten scariest things an earthling can do. It's right up there with eating pigeon heads and . . . well, I'm always trying to make myself brave enough to "speak up," to say something to fellow travelers. It's like a personal challenge. Most of the time it turns out to be a memorable experience. It's one way of reaching through space in a situation where people are usually awkwardly quiet.

Don't think for a single minute that I *always* feel compelled to talk on elevators. No way. Sometimes I don't have enough courage, and sometimes there are circumstances where I sense it wouldn't be appropriate at all. But lots of times I smile just thinking of what I could say! "Did you know that this elevator has a mission statement? It's in the form of a question: 'Need a lift?'"

The more I've thought about this, the more I've been flooded with ideas. And I've "field tested" most of them (with mixed results). I invite you to think with MEE and see if your elevator experiences become more adventurous and more fun. Here are some things you can do and/or say, in no particular order:

One of my favorites is to reach out and touch someone who's getting off and say, "Touched you last!" You'll be amazed at how you can see a whole childhood come flooding back, and the person knows he or she is "It" and tries to get you back as the doors are closing.

There are countless phrases and questions that you can use to "break the ice" on an elevator. How about: "So, is this your first ride?" "Anyone here from out of town?" "Is this as far as you're going?" "Mind if we leave the doors open? I'm claustrophobic." "These aren't real pearls." "Are you my mother?" "Want to know my nickname?" "Is this a freight elevator?" Someone might ask, "Which floor?" and you can respond, "I haven't decided yet, but thanks for asking." Or "I'm not sure—any suggestions?"

Other off-the-wall ideas include questions or statements like "Can you believe how long it's been since we used carrier pigeons?" "What are you doing for Secretary's Day this year?" "If you yawn or laugh, your ears will pop." "I'm here for the marble tournament." "Can you hear that?" Point to your purse, briefcase, or shopping bag and say, "I hope they're not bothering you; they're just thirsty." "I used to be a General." With your ear to the door or wall, "Hey! I think I can hear the ocean!" "Cat got your tongue?" "What do you think I should be?" "My grandpa used to work at Grand Canyon." "What's the best gift anyone ever gave you?" "My brother collects stamps." "I had to choose between fame and fortune." "Sometimes it's as if I can read minds." "I think it would be easier to be a kite than a tractor." "How much wood would a woodchuck chuck if a woodchuck could chuck wood?" "Could I have your autograph?" "Do frogs dream?" "Have you noticed how a little nonsense goes a long, long ways?"

One thing that gets a lot of attention, as I mentioned earlier, is standing facing away from the doors. Handing out paper clips or toothpicks or rubber bands is a personal favorite idea. "We're hoping this new idea will catch on and wanted you to have a sample." One that takes incredible courage is to pretend you're making shadow shapes on the wall or doors, rabbits or dogs or other things. Moving shadows are especially entertaining.

If you feel you don't yet have enough courage to say things out loud, maybe you could try holding a sign (children often enjoy helping you make the sign). "Hello there." "Wheeeeeee." "Don't forget the oil change." "Are you my cousin?" "Fee fi fo fum." "E-I-E-I-O." "Zippity doo-dah." "I can keep a secret." "We're being video-taped." "Whistle while you work." As you feel more confident, you could even have a two-sided sign and keep flipping it over. "Where am I?" / "You are here." "I didn't do it." / "But I know who did." "Starve a fever." / "Starve a cold." "*Why* do the swallows come back to Capistrano?" / "Why did they ever leave?"

One day I got on an elevator in a "field test" frame of

mind. A gentleman got on and was doing his part perfectly. He stood absolutely still, looking straight ahead, and there was no sound besides the mechanical elevator stuff. My heart started to pound. It was clearly time for the field test, but I couldn't think of what I wanted to say. So I said the first thing that came into my mind: "Want to see my paper cut?"

Trying not to smile, he politely said, "No thanks."

My turn again. "That's okay. I don't really have one. I was just trying to think of a way to keep it from being so quiet in here."

He laughed, and we started to talk. He told me about a movie with James Garner in which the whole plot hinged on a paper cut! Something like *36 Hours*. Or maybe only *34 Hours*. But by the time we got off the elevator, we'd had some fun and we were both smiling. By the way, I've seen the movie, and it's pretty good! And James Garner really *did* have a paper cut!

So think with MEE about this. Could we reach out to each other more often? Are there happifying and memorable experiences waiting if we can just have the courage to "break the ice"? Not just on elevators, of course. Maybe never on elevators (maybe you don't have one in your village). I'm just trying to think of all the times when we miss opportunities for connecting with others and perhaps sharing some good cheer and kindness. Let's watch for those and see what we can do to touch each other's lives more!

Being Positive

I've been thinking about being positive.

I had an experience that helped me become more aware of the effect it seems to have on others when people are positive. It was Thursday, March 18, 1999. I was on my way from Salt Lake City to Atlanta. I had boarded the flight, settled down in 23F by the window, swallowed my Dramamine, and shut my eyes. And I was observing. I know observing would seem to be an activity we do with our eyes open, but I was observing with them shut. I was listening and feeling. Seat 23E was unoccupied. A youngish-sounding mother was in 23D on the aisle. Across the aisle was her son Ryan, then his dad in 23B, and a sister by the window in 23A. What I observed was that the mother was trying to get Ryan to sit still and be quiet. The comments went something like this: "Ryan, don't yell!" "Ryan, quit kicking the seat." "Ryan, don't play with your seat belt." "Ryan, quit whining!" "Ryan, don't put your elbows in the aisle." "Ryan, lower your voice!" "Ryan, stop it!"

Ryan sounded about five years old, and it seemed that nothing he did was right. He was curious and fidgety as passengers came down the aisle, and his mother was trying to get him to be polite and quiet. At one point she said something like, "Ry-Ry, do you want to color?" He didn't, but a few minutes later I heard him ask, "Mommy, do you call me Ry-Ry?"

She said, "Yes, sometimes I do."

He was quiet for a few seconds and then said, "I want you to call me Ry-Ry all the time."

I think I figured it out. He liked it when she was positive with him. And in this instance it happened when she called him Ry-Ry instead of Ryan. Could you ever tell when your mother was upset because she used your entire proper name in that certain tone of voice?

Eventually the plane took off and headed east, and Ry-Ry decided he wanted to come and sit in 23E. We had a splendid time all the way to Atlanta. He was in a mood to ask a lot of questions, and I was in a mood to give the most off-the-wall, improbable answers I could think of, complete with funny faces and amazing noises. Ryan's mommy and daddy were both trying to get us to settle down a bit, and we tried. Sort of. But we were on a roll, and the hours went by faster than usual. By the time we got to Atlanta, Ry-Ry was asking if I could go home with them, and he seemed genuinely disappointed that I was going somewhere besides Orlando.

Now it's time to think about this. How do *you* respond when someone is constantly negative toward you and others and life? How does it make you feel when you can't seem to do anything right? And, on the other hand, how do you feel when you're around someone who's usually positive?

Can you think of someone in your life who has waited way too long to hear a positive comment from you? If you really think about this, you're likely to have someone come to mind. Start with your immediate family, and think of each person individually. You may discover that you have a child, a brother or sister, a parent, a grandchild, an aunt or uncle, or someone else who needs to hear something positive from you. And, interestingly, think about yourself. What kinds of messages do you give to yourself? Are you far too negative? I'm just guessing that for too many of us that's the case— we're too hard, too negative, on ourselves. Come up with a couple of true, positive comments—one for you, and one for a friend—and see what happens when you pass them on.

Surprises

've been thinking about surprises.

Specifically, I've been thinking about the kind of surprises Heavenly Father is so good at. We might say "coincidence" when we think of such moments or events, but I don't think that's really true. Let me share one of mine with you and see if it helps you remember some of yours.

On Thursday, March 31, 1994, I was in the Relief Society Building in Salt Lake City. I was helping with the workshops we held as a Relief Society general board right before general conference. Some of us were in one of the offices on the second floor having lunch when one of the secretaries came in and said someone from New York was looking for me. It was a woman from the Philippines, but I didn't recognize her. When she saw me, she came running to me and burst into tears. She hugged and hugged me, and I hugged and hugged her back, and she got lipstick all over my shirt, and we laughed and joked that I was finally "wearing makeup." Then she told me her last name was Valeriano, and it all came back in a flood of memories and tears and love.

This was little Evelyn Valeriano, all grown up. My companion Mary Jane and I had taught her family the gospel in 1964, thirty years earlier, and several had joined the Church. Evelyn was about eleven at the time, and was frustrated and disappointed when she found out her mother was listening to missionaries from another church. Sometimes her mother made her come to our meetings, and she remembered enjoying sitting in front of me and Mary Jane because she could hear us singing. She said, "You always sang second voice [alto]." She recalled the time Mary Jane and I met with her alone to try to help her understand that there should be no ultimatum about her joining a church she knew so little about. We encouraged her to pray to her Heavenly Father and ask Him to help her know if what we were teaching was true. She needed to find out for herself, and she didn't need to be in a hurry.

Evelyn remembered that she hadn't had any experience praying from her heart. She had grown up with specific, memorized prayers. She said when she decided to use her own words, God let her know that it was all true.

She was attending a private Catholic school at the time, and the bus ride took two hours. She began taking her copy of the Book of Mormon with her and reading on her way to and from school. She felt nervous and self-conscious because she was aware of the other children watching her, and she would read and cry and know that the book was true. She made a decision to skip Mass and go to the girls' bathroom at school and hide in the stalls, sitting on the floor, again reading the Book of Mormon. Some of the other girls followed her example of skipping Mass, but they did so to smoke rather than to read.

Eventually one of the women in charge at the school began interviewing each girl to find out what was going on. When it was Evelyn's chance to be interviewed, something inside of her said that even though she was just a young girl, it was time to stand up for what she believed and be honest. So when the sister asked her what was going on, she said: "I've converted and have become a Mormon. I am a member of The Church of Jesus Christ of Latter-day Saints." She said the sister was startled and shocked and said something like, "Oh, my dear child, where did we fail you?"

During all our conversation and remembering, there were many tears and much hugging. There isn't a way to put my feelings into words. Little Evelyn Valeriano, now Marisol, had remained faithful and true through all the years and was Relief Society president in a branch in Brooklyn. She described some of the challenges, saying that "when we go visiting teaching in the projects, we dodge bullets!"

Heavenly Father is so kind, and His surprises are so spectacular. I took Marisol to general conference with me the Sunday after that, and we spent Easter together and promised each other we'd never be separated again. We've kept in touch. She served for several years as Relief Society president in the Brooklyn Stake. During that time, Mary Jane and I went to see her and participated in a couple of meetings and spent a lot of time with her. We were able to see her mother and two of her sisters. And Mary Jane and Marisol met at the Washington, D.C., Temple several times. And now Mary Jane and her mother and Marisol's mother have gone home.

Because Heavenly Father let us be such dear friends here, I feel certain He'll allow us to have some sweet surprises and reunions Over There as well. As I've been thinking about all of this, I've realized that because a lot of these reunions are surprises, it's a good idea to live the best we can so that the reunions will be as sweet as possible.

Miracles

I've been thinking about miracles.

I remember when I was a little girl listening in Sunday School and Primary to stories about Jesus and His miracles. So many things to try to understand! My mother said I came home one Sunday and was looking for a mustard seed—I wanted to go out and see if I could move the Red Hill. I wanted to try to perform a miracle.

There have been miracles in my life. One of the first I remember clearly happened in about 1953. My father was serving as a member of the stake presidency in our town at the time, and that meant that occasionally we had the blessing of having "conference visitors" come to our home for a meal. One Sunday we were to have Elder Mark E. Petersen come, and we were so excited. My father was in meetings with Elder Petersen and others, my mother was fixing dinner, and I was outside playing with my brothers and sisters. My younger sister Susan said she was going to go for a ride on our Shetland pony, Ginger. My little brother Frank, who was just ten years younger than I and "my responsibility," asked me if he could go too. I asked Susan, and she was willing, so I lifted little Frank up behind her and told him to hold on tight.

As I remember it, some neighbor kids threw some rocks, and the pony bucked. I wanted everything to go into slow motion so I could run and catch little Frank as he fell off the back of the pony. I can still remember the sound of his head hitting the sidewalk. I ran and picked him up to take him home. I was afraid he was dying. He was screaming, and I knew he was hurt. I took him to Mom. "Mom, we've killed Frank!" She's a nurse, and she recognized that he was more than merely frightened and bruised. She called Dad and asked him to come home as soon as possible.

I remember that Mom was in the living room holding Frank, who continued to scream. I was waiting with anticipation to see what Dad would do. He's a doctor, and I thought maybe he would call an ambulance or something (although we lived only a block from the hospital). I admit I was almost looking forward to some excitement. I wondered if the police would come and want to interview me and others about the whole incident.

Dad came, and Elder Petersen was with him. They went immediately to see Frank. Dad later told me that he recognized it could be serious. I was watching for him to start doing some of his doctor things. But he first turned to Elder Petersen and said, "Will you help me give a blessing to my son?" He said of course he would, and they exercised their priesthood and gave Frank a blessing. When they finished, he settled down. My mother took him up to his bed, and he went to sleep peacefully. He didn't even go to the hospital. I was young, but I was very impressed with this experience.

Years later, Frank had a mission call and was spending time with friends before leaving. He was with one of our cousins in our Toyota truck (which we called the "Toytillac"), driving up in the canyon near our home in Mapleton. He had come to a stop on a narrow dirt road to make room for a car that was coming the other direction and seemed to be in a hurry. He said all of a sudden he realized he had backed up too far—he was going over the edge.

He said tumbling into that ravine felt like being in a washing machine! There was a tool kit in the cab, and it hit him in the head. When he was brought out of the canyon, he was taken over to the health center at Brigham Young University where our dad was working as a physician. X-rays were taken. There was no damage, but the radiologist said to Dad, "Come and take a look at this old suture line." There was the evidence that years earlier Frank had suffered a basal skull fracture when he fell off the pony. And he had been healed by a priesthood blessing given by my father and a wonderful Church leader, Elder Petersen. I felt an increased sense of gratitude and awareness about the power that is part of all that it means to have men called of God to serve and bless us. It was a miracle.

Think of the miracles in your own life. Perhaps there hasn't been anything like what I've described here, but I know there have been miracles. Have you seen a brand-new baby or a sunflower up close? Have you seen the sun rise and set? Have you tried counting stars on a dark, clear night (especially if you're in the wilderness and not in a city)? Have you had prayers answered? Have you felt loved and forgiven?

Visiting

I've been thinking about visiting.

Has anyone ever come to visit you at a time when it made such a difference? Maybe the visit was planned, or maybe it was unexpected, but think of a visit that you needed and how much it meant.

I want to share something that happened to me on Sunday, April 16, 2000. About a month before that I had received a letter from a woman in Ogden named Marlene, telling me of her frequent visits to Ruby Dickson. Ruby was in a care center in South Ogden and had ALS—Lou Gehrig's disease. This woman had been reading a book of mine to Ruby and said they had both enjoyed it very much. Ruby told her about being in the MTC years earlier with her husband. She said they'd enjoyed their classes with me. And then she said, "Oh, I wish she were my friend!" So this woman wrote to tell me that, and she said that although she knew I was very busy, she kept getting a feeling she should write and tell me about Ruby. She said she knew that if I could ever go and visit Ruby, it would be a blessing for me, not just for Ruby.

When I first got the letter, I was thinking "no way." I admit it. I was so very seldom near Ogden. There was way too much to do. I was too busy. The BYU Women's Conference was coming soon, and I had a huge assignment with a service event plus a talk. Whine whine whine.

Then, on this particular Sunday in April, I was driving home from Idaho Falls, not in any particular hurry. I had left earlier than I'd thought I could, so it was only about 9:30 in the morning by the time I reached the Utah-Idaho border, and a thought came into my mind: *How about visiting Ruby today?* Then I thought, *Shucks! Why didn't I bring the letter with me!* I just hadn't thought about it ahead of time. But then the still small voice came into my mind, almost with a little "nyeh nyeh nyeh nyeh" feel to it. (It cracked me up!) "The letter's in the trunk."

Oh! Yes! I had taken letters with me to Idaho Falls, thinking I would go through them. They were in the trunk! I pulled off the first off-ramp, opened the trunk, and found the letter. I was smiling happily! Back on the freeway, I headed for Ogden. The address was about 1050 East and 5500 South, and I seemed to take just the right route to find it without any trouble at all. I was beginning to realize Someone was helping.

In I went, not knowing where Ruby was at all. And, perhaps because it was Sunday, there was no one at the information desk. So I wandered a bit until I found a worker. I asked her where Ruby's room was, and she told me which direction to go. The place was *huge*. I walked past a dining room and realized they were having sacrament meeting there. I was sorry I hadn't arrived sooner, because I really wanted to partake of the sacrament. But I kept going. When I got to the area where the worker had said Ruby's room was, I asked another worker about it, and she told me where it was but said, "Ruby's in sacrament meeting." So I said I would wait. I walked back down the hall.

Then I saw two cute young deacons coming my direction (they looked about nine!), walking with a woman who had a list. I caught on—they were taking the sacrament to people who had requested it but who couldn't get out of their beds or rooms to go to the meeting. So I asked, "Can I be on your list?" And the woman instantly said, "Of course!" and one of the deacons held the trays so I could get bread and then water, and I was able to partake of the sacrament. That meant so much to me!

I continued back down the hall, found a chair, and pulled it near the door of the dining room so I could hear what was being said. I couldn't see a place to sit inside. I took a few notes as I listened. Then they started to sing the closing hymn ("Love at Home"), so I put the chair back and went to wait in Ruby's room. As I walked back down the hall and turned a corner, there was a woman sitting in a chair in the hallway. I smiled at her and said "hello" or "good morning" or something like that.

With all kinds of joy, excitement, and anticipation she looked at me and asked, "Do you know me?"

I said, "I'd like to—what's your name?" I took her hands in mine. She said her name was Elizabeth. I wished her a happy day and a Happy Easter. I was feeling that there were so many people like Elizabeth who have forgotten who they are and seem to live without much awareness of where they are. And why.

After a brief visit with Elizabeth, I went on to Ruby's room. I looked at the pictures and things she had hanging around. I got some impressions of who she was just from looking at what was important enough to her to have it in the room. Pictures of her family and the Savior. A couple of beautiful quilts. Some other handwork. A copy of the latest visiting teaching message. Then someone brought her in. She was in a wheelchair, and it looked like a brother from the sacrament meeting (not a worker, and not another patient) had brought her back. She had him position her so that her "call button" was underneath her two strongest fingers. Her ALS had progressed to the point where she was basically a quadriplegic, unable to move from the neck down, but she was very cheerful about helping him to know what to do to help her be correctly positioned.

I was over near her window at the time, and she was looking at me with all kinds of curiosity. She obviously didn't recognize me from having met me many years ago. When the brother left, I went and sat on her bed beside her, and she asked with kind of a puzzled expression, "Should I know you?" Or maybe it was more like, "I don't think I know you."

I said, "Well I don't know you either, but I came to visit you anyway. I'm Mary Ellen Edmunds."

She looked hard at me and said, "*Who?*" (as if she couldn't believe it). I told her again. She kind of squealed. "The General! I can't believe it!"

I said, "I can't either!" and we laughed. She got the "General" part from my childhood war stories. Ha. We had a wonderful visit. I stayed almost two hours and loved it. We had such a *good* time together. Ruby was eighty-two, much older than most ALS victims. She said she was by far the oldest member in her support group. She had a delightful sense of humor, a bright mind, and was so interesting and easy to talk to. She told me she had had a party for some of the workers one evening, complete with a video and popcorn. Not long before that, two of her granddaughters had taken her to the Ogden Temple. She said she knew she would feel closer there to her husband, who had passed away, so she very much wanted to go. She told me she knew she wouldn't live much longer, and that she didn't mind. She said she had given everything away.

When I returned home I sent her a surprise box with another book, a tape, and some nonsense things. I thanked her for the visit—for enriching my day and my life. I got another letter from Marlene letting me know that Ruby had gone Home. I felt so thankful that I had stopped that day—that the idea to do so had come, that I "just happened" to have her letter in the car, and that I was able to spend such a wonderful two hours with her.

Can you think of someone who needs a visit from you? Maybe you can't go there today or soon, but could you make a phone call or send a note? Try not to miss too many of these chances to lift and be lifted.

Wasps

I've been thinking about wasps.

I don't like them. They annoy me, and they make me nervous. I admit that in all the years I've lived in my home in Mapleton, I've only had one wasp sting, but wow, did it hurt! I go nuts when a wasp gets inside the house and is flying around. I know it's going to attack me any minute.

Often wasps build *huge* nests around my house. I remember a guy taking the cover off my electricity meter and jumping off the ladder because the inside was full of nests and wasps! Yuk! More than once there's been a nest in my mailbox on the corner of my street! Once I discovered there must be a big nest between the sliding doors, because I killed about fifty (yes, fifty!) young wasps on one single day! Someone invented those spray cans that can shoot wasp killer twelve or fifteen feet, and I've had some feel-good experiences where I've walked around the house shooting at nests. Once there was one the size of a softball in the corner of one of the windows! I cringed, thinking of all the little wasps being manufactured inside! I have almost a phobia about spiders and bugs and wasps and that kind of thing.

Then, a few years ago I had an experience that changed my thinking. One afternoon there were two wasps flying around between the sliding doors (one of the places where I seem to have a constant problem with them). What I usually do is squish them with a shoe. I got to one, and I hit it sort of "sideways" so that it slid under the metal cover for the glass door—trapped in there and "writhing." I didn't think too much about it. I knew it would die soon. I didn't get the other one, but I wasn't concerned. *Let 'em suffer! They're out to get me! They're the enemy!*

A while later I was looking out the window, not thinking about anything in particular, and certainly not thinking about the wasps. But then I noticed there was a wasp by the wounded, dying one (probably dead by then). It had its head right by the other head. It was motionless. I stood still, looking, and I can't explain it, but a feeling of tenderness and compassion came over me. I felt *sad.* I felt a deeply sad feeling of regret and remorse—partly that I'd tried to kill the wasp, and partly that I hadn't put it out of its suffering when it got stuck. It made me sick. Sorry. Ashamed.

You might have to think for quite a while to understand what I'm trying to say in all of this. The whole experience caught me off guard and caused me to think for a long, long time. I remembered reading a book by Albert Schweitzer about the holiness of every living thing, and I do believe that all living things have some kind of soul, some kind of feelings. I don't pretend to know what they are, what a wasp or a tree or a flower might think or feel, but it's enough for me to know they're alive. They are *living things*. God created them. Sunflowers turn to His sun in the sky each day and follow it through. Even plants respond to attention, kindness, good music, encouraging words, enough water, and all.

I go so far as to speak to and develop friendships with inanimate things. I do. My car, my home, books. . . . Oh, that's enough, I guess. Maybe I'm just inviting you to think of an experience you might have had where a helpless insect—a "sworn enemy"—ended up teaching you an important lesson or brought feelings to your heart that were tenderizing. Maybe my experience with the wasps caused me to think more than I had for a long time about having a reverence for life, for all life. Could we be more careful? More respectful? I'm not just talking about wasps or bugs or something, but about all life.

Keeping Promises

I've been thinking about keeping promises.

Someone once told me that I should make promises very, very carefully and then be sure to keep them, especially promises to myself and to God. Several years ago I had an assignment with my dear friend MarJean in Pocatello, Idaho. I had almost asked someone else to take the assignment for me because I wasn't feeling very well at the time. (I think I had a dead battery, or maybe I had just run out of gas). But I felt strongly that I wanted to go. We had a training meeting and dinner on Friday evening, a breakfast, lunch, and dinner on Saturday, and three women's conferences.

I'm sharing this much detail about our schedule because I want to say that by the time we finished the Saturday evening meeting we were pretty worn out. After that last meeting, a woman came up to me and said, "Connie wanted to be here but wasn't feeling well."

Connie was someone I had known since my growing-up days in Cedar City. Her father was our high school principal. When Connie was a senior in high school, my mom taught her home nursing class. Then Connie was one of my favorite nursing instructors while I was at BYU. Later we taught together for several years. We had remained good friends for all the years since.

I knew Connie lived in Orem, so I said to the woman in Pocatello, "But she doesn't live here." She said that Connie had broken her foot, and that her sister-in-law, this woman's daughter, was caring for her. I asked if I could please get an address or a phone number. She said, "Oh, you're much too busy." That frustrated me. I don't like to seem too busy for things that matter as much as this did. So I asked again, and she wrote the address down. I thanked her.

I couldn't get Connie off my mind. The next morning after sacrament meeting I asked MarJean if she would mind delaying our trip home for an extra hour so we could find Connie. She said she didn't mind at all. We looked in the phone book and figured out about where she was from the map. I didn't want to call because I was afraid she wouldn't let me come. She had seemed to be kind of a lonely person. Both her parents had passed away, and then her only brother, Gordon, died unexpectedly of a heart attack. So she was pretty much alone and sometimes didn't seem to want visitors.

We found the place, and her sister-in-law's new husband let us in. He said he didn't know if she'd want to see us. (I was thinking the same thing.) I said, "Please tell her it's Mary Ellen, and we'll just stay a few minutes." Well, she let us visit! I felt so grateful. I sat by her on her bed and hugged and kissed her and she cried and it was wonderful. I felt like it was the reason I went to Pocatello, just to find her and visit her and hopefully lift her spirits a little.

I wrote her a letter when I got back. Then, a few days later, I heard from her sister-in-law saying Connie was very ill and was in the LDS Hospital and might have to have her foot amputated. I went to see her as soon as possible. She had found out years before that she was a diabetic, and without realizing it she had gotten an infection underneath the cast from her broken foot. Even with massive doses of antibiotics, the infection couldn't be stopped, and she had her foot amputated. I went to see her every week in Salt Lake. We had marvelous visits. We shared so many things, so many memories of thirty years earlier when she was my instructor and we were in a much smaller LDS Hospital.

Once when I went to see her she'd been moved to another floor, and I had quite a search before I found her. I walked in and said (so often, things like this come out of my mouth before I realize how they sound), "You can hide, but you cannot run." Well, we had a good laugh—thank goodness she had a sense of humor—and another wonderful visit. I read her one of my favorite stories, "The Happy Prince," by Oscar Wilde, and I told her I'd see her the next Saturday.

That Saturday came and I had talks to give up near Ogden. I did quite a bit of visiting afterward, working my way from Ogden to about 7500 South in Salt Lake. While I was visiting some friends there, I remembered that I had promised Connie I would come to see her. It was late in the afternoon by then, I was tired, and the LDS Hospital was way back up at the other end of the valley. But the still small voice whispered: "You promised."

So back up I went, and I'm so thankful I did. She was watching for me. She knew I would come. I stayed quite a while as nurses and others came and went, changing dressings, trying to get her to breathe more deeply (they seemed concerned she wasn't getting enough oxygen). We had such a good time. Before I left I said to her, "You know, I'm really quite a silly person, but beneath all of this I really, really love you and care about you. I think of you, pray for you, put your name in the temple and all." And she responded with love and gratitude and said she didn't know what she'd do without me. I left, thanking Heavenly Father over and over again for caring enough to give me that prompting, for reminding me I'd made a promise.

Imagine how I felt when I found out that Connie passed away the following Tuesday evening. I shuddered to think how I'd have felt if I hadn't gone back on Saturday—if I'd thought something like, "Oh, I'll go next week. She'll understand." Because of that feeling that came into my heart—"but you promised"—I haven't had to live with an "if only" feeling.

Think about promises you've made. Sometimes we don't use that word, but we'll say something like "I'll be there," or "You can count on me," or "I'll drop by on my way home," or "I'll call you on Sunday." Can you think of having said things to someone who's still waiting for you to keep your promise? I guess the advice I mentioned at the beginning of this little chapterette is still good counsel: Make promises very carefully, and be sure to keep them. Especially promises to yourself and to God.

Christmas

I've been thinking about Christmas, and the magic of Christmas.

I try to do things to help myself and others feel the wonderful spirit of Christmas. Several years ago I had a dear friend give me some money to give away. I went to the bank and got "brand-new" money, a total of $400. I put it into eight different envelopes, each containing a $20, two $10's, and two $5's. Then I put a note in with each one:

"MERRY CHRISTMAS! Yes, this is money. Real money. Not much . . . but a little extra to help you have (it is hoped) a happier holiday. The one who shares wishes to remain anonymous but sends along a wish that the coming year will be one of the best ever for you and those you love. NUMBERS 6:24–26—'The Lord bless thee, and keep thee: The Lord make his face shine upon thee, and be gracious unto thee: The Lord lift up his countenance upon thee, and give thee peace.' He lives. He loves you. Joy to the world! Again, MERRY CHRISTMAS!"

Next I called two of my nieces. Katie had just turned sixteen and Tina was almost thirteen. I asked, "What are you doing Friday afternoon?" This was just a few days before Christmas. Each was free, so I said I'd pick them up around 1:00 P.M., and we were going to go have a Christmas adventure. They were so curious and excited!

I picked up Tina first, and then we went to get Katie. I showed them the decorated envelopes and had them look to see what was inside and asked them to read one of the notes. Then they *really* started to get excited!! I told them a kind person had donated this money, and we were going to help her give it away to some people who needed an extra something at Christmastime. Next I asked them where people went to shop for groceries who had to pinch pennies, who had to shop very carefully and didn't have extra money to spend. After some thought, they named a store, and I said, "That's where we're going."

I explained that each of them would have four envelopes to give away to someone who needed what was inside. Their eyes were getting a bit tear-filled by this time! We talked about "criteria," and they came up with great ideas, such as looking for people who were buying basics rather than the more expensive prepared foods, and people who were using a list, and parents who had children with them, and so on. They said they wanted to look at the way people were dressed and whether they had on a lot of makeup (I found that so interesting). I loved being with them and listening to their discussion and joining in their absolute excitement at this great Christmas adventure, compliments of my friend, a genuine Saint.

Eventually we also decided that the best thing we could do was to ask Heavenly Father to help us find those who needed the most help. So we had a little prayer together before leaving. We talked about what they should say when they gave the envelope to someone. We realized that unless they said something, the person might just think it was an ad or a promotion, and they might throw it away! So they decided to say something like, "You've been chosen to receive a little extra something for Christmas, and we hope what's in this envelope will make your holidays even happier. God bless you." Isn't that good?

We got to the designated store and parked in the

"nethermost parts of the parking lot" and began wandering around out there. Katie spied our first "mark." It was a woman just coming out, and she had a basket full of necessities and two children, with two other children running beside her. One of the little ones in the basket was screaming her head off, and the mother was trying to push the basket while calming her baby. Katie went up to her (while Tina and I hid behind a car) and handed her an envelope and said her little part, and then came back to us. The mother stood looking kind of puzzled and then smiled and continued to her car. And that was the beginning of our beautiful, unforgettable Christmas adventure.

Sometimes we would go inside the store and sit on a bench where we could watch people checking out, and we'd discuss different ones, trying to determine if they were the right ones. We were all praying in our hearts, of course. Tina found one woman who had a cast on her leg and was giving directions to her children from a wheelchair as they bought their stuff. Later, after she discovered what was in the envelope, we could see her looking for us, but we hid so that she couldn't find us, even though she saw us a couple of times.

Once when we were inside the store, back by where

the milk, veggies, and fruits were (we again felt that perhaps those who were buying the real stuff instead of the more expensive "ready-made" would be more in need), one of the store workers who had apparently seen us roaming and sneaking around came up and asked if he could help us. He was looking quite suspicious, we thought. (And I'm sure he thought *we* looked suspicious!) I said to him in a whisper, "No, we don't need your help, but thanks for asking. We're *elves,* and we're here on *official business!*" He was so funny after that! He kept saying "Shhhhhhh" and "carry on" and similar things. It was too good to be true!

Well, we eventually gave away all eight envelopes, and we had incredible feelings in our hearts. I have to tell about another one specifically. We were back out in the parking lot, and Katie spied a young mother, probably in her early thirties, who was out on a bench near the front doors of the store. She had a basket with very little in it, and she had six children gathered around her, probably six, five, four, three, two, and one (that's how old they looked). She was giving each of them a bag to carry. One had two loaves of bread. From what we could tell, it seemed she had purchased only what she really needed, and only what they could carry. This touched our hearts deeply. She and the children were dressed very simply, even humbly.

So we kept watching. When she'd given out the few bags, she took the cart way back to the front of the store (which impressed us further). Katie approached her and gave her the envelope and shared her little message. Then the three of us hid behind one of the posts near the entrance of the store where we could watch without being discovered. This sweet mother looked at the pretty envelope for a while, and then carefully opened it. She took the note and the money out and sat looking just stunned, as if she couldn't believe it. She looked up in our direction, and we quickly hid further behind the post. She sat and slowly read the note, looking overcome with the wonder of it . . . the surprise. Carefully she put everything back in the envelope and then looked up again. We quickly hid. She started after us! We started to run! She called out, "I can see you running! Stop right where you are!" And we did.

She approached us, fighting her tears. First she "melted" in my arms, and I hugged and hugged her and kissed her, and the tears came. Then she hugged both Tina and Katie (who also started to cry), and then hugged me again. She just kept saying, "Thank you, oh, *thank you.*" And she said, "You don't know . . . you have no idea . . ." Something like that. And then she turned and went away. We just stood there, wiping our tears and feeling quite overcome with feelings of love and the sweet joy that comes with sharing. As we talked about her over and over, we were wishing we had given her all eight envelopes. We went to see if we could find her, but she had gone. We sat on "her" bench, wishing we could do more for her. We had no idea who she was or where she lived or anything.

Then we got an idea. Heavenly Father knew who she was and where she lived (duh!). So we decided we would all three include her in our prayers, and that we would ask Heavenly Father to prompt someone—a neighbor or whomever—to do a "Sub for Santa" for her, or something special for Christmas.

Well, we had a most remarkable time together. We'll never forget it. Never. Tina said, "Well, I sure have my testimony ready for next month!" We all kept talking about how *good* we felt inside, how tender, and how much our experience had meant to us. When we got to Katie's, we went down to her bedroom and had a thank-you prayer. Heavenly Father was so good to us on that beautiful Friday afternoon. The three of us still talk about that special Christmas adventure we shared.

Has this brought some of your own memories back to you? Of course, it doesn't take $400 to have something similar happen. Maybe you helped with a "Sub for Santa." Maybe you're remembering when you gave part (or all) of what you'd have spent on gifts for each other to do something for someone who needed it more. In addition to memories, have any ideas come to you? Ideas about what you might do not just at Christmastime, but anytime? Much of the joy is in the planning. (I was going to say "plotting," but it didn't feel or sound quite right.) This could be a great discussion for a family council, or a talk among neighbors or friends. Don't miss the chance for joy!

Imprisoned

I've been thinking about being imprisoned.

One of my favorite passages in the New Testament is in the book of Matthew, toward the end of the Savior's earthly ministry. It is the account of those who are invited to be on His right hand because they have responded when He's been in need. One of the things mentioned is, "I was in prison, and ye came unto me" (Matthew 25:36).

That particular phrase was much on my mind on Sunday, May 2, 1999. I was driving toward the Utah State Prison, having been asked to present a fireside in one of the men's sections there. Oh, my goodness . . . I had never even *been* there, let alone had *any* understanding of what it must be like to be there all day every day for years. I admit I had "butterflies." I prayed a *lot*.

That day I took Mom to her ward to sacrament meeting, and I said, "Let's go to church together one more time before I go to prison," and we laughed. But I was really concerned about this fireside. I wanted what I said to be *right,* to be something meaningful and honest. I remember that as I was driving toward the prison I was thinking again about the phrase in Matthew, and I was talking to Heavenly Father about that. I said something like, "Your son is in prison, and I'm going to visit him. What do you want me to say?" What a tender feeling!

I got there early, and some of the inmates arrived, found a couple of guitars, and were singing some songs they'd written. They were all about Jesus. I was deeply moved. I also saw one of their Family History libraries in a classroom there as part of the Marvin J. Ashton chapel. I was told there was an even bigger place in the main area of the prison, and they submitted more names for temple work than almost any other single location. This seemed to me so symbolic and sweet—to have people who were in prison working to "free" those who were in another kind of prison, waiting for ordinances to be performed for them in the temple. We sang "How Great Thou Art," and I was sitting on the stand in the small chapel, looking and listening as the men sang these beautiful words. I was so touched by everything that was happening. Brother Robert was asked to offer the opening prayer, and once again it was "tenderizing" in a very powerful way. He shared what he was feeling so honestly and sweetly.

When it was time for me to speak, I shared from my heart. There was nothing else I could do or wanted to do because of all I was feeling. I started out by telling them that we had the same Heavenly Father, and that He loved us very much, and that I was their sister, and they were my brothers. Then I just went from there. I asked how many of them had children, and at least half of them raised their hands. So for part of my time I spoke about relationships, and how they might be strengthened. I shared many of my own experiences and what I felt I had learned. I spoke for about an hour and twenty minutes, and it flew by. We laughed, we shed a few tears together, and when I went to finish I told them again that they were my brothers and I was their sister, and that I was honored to be with them. The tears came as I told them, "I love you, my brothers." I really meant it.

Then a brother who has helped them make a CD played three of their original songs, and on the last one, called "Calvary," he asked those in the choir to come up and sing along with the CD. Well, that pretty much knocked me over completely (I'd been "tipping" all evening), and I never quite recovered. I can't describe the feeling as I watched and listened and *felt*. I wish I knew the words. But here were these men, in their inmate clothing with numbers stamped on them and "UDC INMATE" on everything, sitting, standing, singing from their hearts. It was a deeply moving, permanently wonderful opportunity.

I will never be or feel the same. It's a way different experience for me now as I go over the "Point-of-the-Mountain," driving past the Utah State Prison. I know that many of these men will just keep coming back to prison—one of the volunteers pointed out that the man who offered the closing prayer was back for his fourth experience behind bars—but that wasn't what I was thinking about. I felt a genuine sense of caring and love for them, knowing that was what I was there for. I didn't have to judge, or wonder what they did to be imprisoned, or wonder if they were repentant. I was just sent to be kind.

As I continued thinking about the experience, and also about the phrase from Matthew, I remembered something that happened to me while I was a student nurse working in public health. One of my patients was a teenage girl with cerebral palsy. I'll call her Cindy. I had visited a few times, and her mother was always there. She wouldn't let Cindy say anything; she would answer every question. Even when I'd look directly at Cindy and ask her the question, before she could even try to formulate an answer, her mother would quickly respond.

One day when I went to visit I could tell no one was home but Cindy. I could hear her on the other side of the door, trying to get it open. Eventually I got in, and we had a wonderful conversation about school, classes she was taking, some of her frustrations, the loneliness she sometimes felt when she wanted to be friends but could feel others making fun of her. She talked to me about math in particular. She said that because of her cerebral palsy she couldn't write very well or very quickly, so she had become able to work out solutions to most math problems in her mind. She said, though, that the teacher would rarely call on her because he had a hard time understanding her answers.

I thought about Cindy being imprisoned in a body that didn't work very well. And from what she said and what I observed, it seemed that there were more opportunities to "come unto her" than any of us had realized.

Can you think of anyone who might be imprisoned? Perhaps it's someone who's homebound because of illness or disability. Perhaps it's someone who spends most of the time at home because he or she can't drive anymore (or never could). Maybe it's someone who's actually in a prison or some other kind of institution. It could even be someone who's imprisoned by an addiction or bad habit or something like that. If we think deeply about what the Savior said in Matthew 25, we just might come to a realization that there are many who are imprisoned in a wide variety of circumstances, and that there may be more ways to "come unto them" than we had realized. A note, a phone call, a visit, a little gift, an earnest prayer . . . if we each do what we can do, those who are imprisoned may feel they've been found and noticed and loved as they seldom have before.

Spontaneity

I've been thinking about spontaneity.

I consider myself a rather spontaneous person, and it can (and has) caused me a lot of trouble. But it has also brought me some pretty wonderful moments as well.

I want to take you with me to Lawton, Oklahoma, March 1995, where I had an assignment with the "Know Your Religion" program. I arrived at the chapel early and, after checking in with those in charge, I sat in the foyer and watched people come in. Oh, I love doing that! I enjoy being "anonymous," just sitting there unobserved, getting some idea about who the people are. Some young people came. One of the first was with her parents and didn't look too thrilled to be there. I caught her eye and motioned for her to come over where I was sitting. "Did they make you come?" I asked. She kind of laughed and said yes, having no idea who I was, of course. I said, "Well, look, if this talk gets boring, let's get out of there."

At first she looked at me like I couldn't be serious, but then she laughed and said okay. I had her shake my hand to make it a deal. I told her to give me a signal after fifteen minutes or so if the talk was boring, and we would cut out. She had a cute accent and was so much fun. She went into the chapel but then came back out again and we talked some more. Her name was Christy. She was sixteen years old. I asked her about her school jacket, and she told me of their football team and all. We talked again about leaving after fifteen or twenty minutes, and we gave each other a "high-five." She went back in the chapel.

When I finally went in there and sat up on the stand, I looked for Christy. I found her sitting to my right on the side, leaning on the wall. When she saw me, I watched as she slowly sat up, in disbelief that I was sitting on the stand. I could almost read her mind: "She's not the speaker, is she? Maybe she's going to give the opening prayer. . . ." It was hilarious! I was "cracking up" inside with the fun of it.

When I got up, I said something like, "Brothers and sisters, this might be a very short evening for you. Christy and I have a deal [and instantly her parents looked over at her with a look that said, 'What have you done?'].

We're not in the mood to be bored. We're giving this talk about fifteen minutes, and then, if it's boring, we're out of here!" Everyone in the audience seemed to get it, and we were having a good time.

I started speaking, keeping a watch on my little clock. After about fifteen minutes, I put my hand up to the mike (as if to pretend that no one else would be able to hear what I was saying) and whispered, "Christy! What do you think?" She was dying, kind of shaking her head like, "I can't believe this is really happening to me."

I asked, "Should we stay for the whole talk?" and I was still "whispering" with my hand up by the mike. She nodded yes and gave me a "thumbs up," so I announced to everyone that Christy and I were staying. And I finished my talk.

When the meeting was finished, Christy hurried past her parents and up to the stand, and I hugged and hugged her and thanked her for letting me tease her a bit in public. She kept saying things like, "I learned a lot!" I could see her parents smiling at me and saying, "Thank you!" I really enjoyed that chance just to be spontaneous and do something unexpected. It would have been fun to keep in touch with Christy and find out more about her (and get her side of the story). All I can tell you is that everyone seemed to have responded positively, and I think Christy ended up being glad she came.

Can you think of a time when you've felt like doing or saying something, but you just didn't have the courage, or you weren't in the mood? Do you think we might miss some important and meaningful connections if we fail to be spontaneous, to respond to good ideas that come to our minds and our hearts? I've always felt that spontaneity was a sign of hope. What do you think about that? Both spontaneity and creativity—along with other qualities, of course—are signs of hope, of looking forward, of happy anticipation.

The Solar System

I've been thinking about the solar system.

It's big. It's really, really big. People sing about planets, stars, the moon, the sun, and the Milky Way. I heard that women are from Venus and men are from Mars. I think I'm from Pluto. I've always had nice feelings about Pluto. I'm glad the effort to get it demoted to a nonplanet wasn't successful. I've already lost way too much from fourth grade, and I didn't want to lose Pluto, too!

Sensitivity

I've been thinking about sensitivity a lot.

What a wonderful quality! Sensitivity includes an empathy or awareness of others' feelings, circumstances, and such. One morning in April 1994 I was teaching a group of senior missionaries. The topic was helping others come back to full participation in the Church. We shared ideas with each other about why people go away, and why they come back, and what we can do to help. One woman raised her hand and shared a story that made me cry. She said that when she was a lot younger, her husband was called as a member of a bishopric. She was advised that it would probably be best for her not to have a calling during his years of service. This would make it possible for her to spend time with her children and to be supportive of her husband. So that's what she did. She was released from what she'd been doing and focused on her family. She told us how much she looked forward to receiving a calling once her husband was released from the bishopric.

Eventually her husband's release came, and she waited with great anticipation for the chance to have a calling and to serve in the ward again. She had missed being involved in that way. Time went by, but she wasn't called to do anything specific. She said she felt kind of discouraged—she wanted to be involved, and she wanted to feel like she belonged. Finally she went to talk to the new bishop. She asked him about it, wondering if there was some reason why she hadn't received a calling. She said he told her, "No one has asked for you." *Ouch!* It hurt even to hear it all these years later, and it still brought tears to her just in the remembering. She told us that if she hadn't been strong in her faith she might have stayed home, feeling she was neither needed nor wanted. "If I'm not needed, then why come? If no one wants me . . ."

President Hinckley has said that people need three things in order to stay close to the Church and strong in their faith. One of these is something to do: a calling, a responsibility. Can you think of a way you can help make that happen in your sphere of influence? And can you think of someone specifically who might be feeling left out or not needed?

Obedience

I've been thinking about obedience.

I've been taught since I was a little person that blessings come from obeying God's commandments. I've come to know that this also applies to following counsel from our Church leaders. One thing we've been advised to do for many years is to be prepared, and this includes having a supply of food on hand. Food storage has been emphasized by many prophets (including Joseph in Egypt). President Ezra Taft Benson said on at least three different occasions, "The revelation to produce and store food may be as essential to our temporal welfare today as boarding the ark was to the people in the days of Noah" (*Ensign,* November 1980, 33).

In 1992, my friend Joy told about an experience she had in Tennessee where she and her husband served their mission. She told of a family in their branch who were fixing up an old home. Temporarily, they put their food storage in the attic. One of the children in the family, a twelve-year-old girl, slept in a room right below the attic. The rest of the family slept in rooms on a lower floor. In the middle of the night, the young girl heard popcorn popping in the attic, then bottles breaking. She realized there was a fire and awakened everyone else. Although all their belongings were lost in the fire, the family made it out safely, thanks to popcorn popping in the attic and a little girl who was awakened and realized what was happening.

Maybe you and I don't have stories quite so dramatic about how our food storage has helped us, but many of us can tell of times when illness or the loss of a job or some other circumstance has made it very important to have extra food and other supplies on hand. Obedience brings blessings. I've been thinking that much of the time we're probably not even aware of the blessings we receive for our faithfulness—those blessings aren't always dramatic or spectacular. But we *are* blessed. I'm convinced of that.

Simplifying

I've been thinking about simplifying.

I've been thinking about this for a long, long time, and every once in a while I make some progress in simplifying my own life. I get rid of a few boxes and sacks, some books, a few items of clothing, and other varied items.

And then came the day when simplifying was forced upon me without warning. On October 31, 2000, I pulled out of the driveway on my way to the airport to spend a week in California. At about that same moment, a little plug or valve popped off a pipe under the kitchen sink. For the entire week, hot water sprayed forth, going from the kitchen to here and there and everywhere, running and dripping on treasures and junk, upstairs and down.

I got home on Tuesday, November 7. As I backed into the garage, I noticed the window on the door into the house was wet. Half my brain began playing the theme music to *Psycho* (remember the violins?), and the other half started going numb trying to think of a different/good reason for a wet window. I had to push hard several times to get the door open. It was swollen. And then I heard it—the sound of water. The sound of *lots* of water . . . spraying, running, falling, dripping. I think that's about the time I went into shock.

I walked around on the squishy, soaked carpets as if in a bad, bad dream. The whole place was a steam bath. Eventually I went down to the basement, over squishy, wet carpet again, and got the water main turned off. That didn't stop the running and dripping for quite a while. I realized my feet were wet and cold at that point, so I got my snow boots out of the closet (they were wet inside too, like everything else in the place), put them on, went back out to the car, and drove over to Mom's place. I had stopped at the BYU Creamery to get her some cream, and I put it in her fridge, and then I went and sat down and said, "I've had a flood." Neither of us wanted to believe that what I had just said out loud was true.

After a while I called the insurance company, they got me in touch with a "restoration" guy (he said no, his company didn't have anything to do with what happened in 1820), and I met him and his wife back at the flood site. As we walked around, I kept discovering new places where water had ruined something. Some family members dropped by to help haul things to the few places in the basement that had remained dry.

Then everyone left. I was alone. In one of the most ridiculous of my actions, I had decided I had to stay there that night. *What?* Yes. It was as if my home and everything in it had been wounded, and I wanted to be there to give comfort. Even now I can't really explain it. *Everything* was wet or damp, including my mattress and bedding and all the clothing in my closet. I had to dig in my suitcase to find something dry. And then I got in my wet, cold bed and . . . and turned on the electric blanket! It's a wonder I didn't kill myself. As I look back on it, I'm positive angels had to be pulled in off P-day and got a lot of overtime that night. . . .

The next day the insurance claims guy arrived, and we began looking through more of the damaged stuff. And the long, *slow* process of taking things apart and putting them back together began.

The next weeks and months were pretty much a nightmare. There were huge fans everywhere, upstairs and down, and dehumidifiers and ozone machines. The level of noise was unbearable—oh, the noise noise noise *noise!* I was home just one day, then off to Arizona for three days of "Know Your Religion." Home for three days and then to North Carolina for a women's conference. Home two days and then to California for a week. I would come home to find carpets and floors torn up, drapes gone (ruined). Eventually the entire kitchen was gone, right to the wall. I called my brother Frank, who's an optometrist, and told him something was wrong with my eyes: I couldn't see my kitchen! It had been there, but it wasn't there anymore!

At some point I asked the insurance guy, "How bad was this flood?" and he said, "In the top five." I actually felt a tiny little thrill at that—I had finally reach the top five in something!

But the whole ordeal was quite traumatic. One day the restoration guy said to me something like, "You'll be so happy with the way things turn out. It'll be like having a brand-new home." I said I'd been happy and content with the way it was. And that was true.

While all this was going on, I moved over to stay with my mother for about four months. We told everyone we were bonding. She was so kind to me. And that's true for many other family members and neighbors and friends.

So now I'll say some magic words (because they're true): It could have been worse. (Whenever my sister Charlotte is around and I say that, she says, "Yes—it could have been *my* house!") It could have been a fire. It could have happened before Mapleton residents got hooked up to the sewer. (I shudder to think of what the basement would have been like had the water not found a drain.) My missionary journals were spared (one got wet, but not ruined). The beautiful painting of the Savior that my brother-in-law Wendell did for me was not damaged (even though almost everything else hanging on walls did have water damage from the condensation). And on and on. It would have been a lot worse without the incredible help from so many friends. I hope I can follow their examples of kindness and generosity.

I need to admit that it was hard to see some of my "stuff and things" hauled off—things I thought I couldn't do without, like unfinished projects that I would certainly get to "any minute"—maybe next year. But now they were spoiled, and they were being put in cars and trucks and taken to the dump.

I survived. After all, they were just *things*. Stuff and

things. And am I not the person who speaks so often about materialism? I have to say that I've been pleased I haven't been hysterical about all of this. It makes me think maybe I've made a *little* bit of progress in my attempts at simplifying my life and trying not to set my heart so much on "stuff and things." What do you think?

Sharing

I've been thinking about sharing.

When I think of a great example of sharing, I think of Mary and Dayne and something that happened at Christmastime in 2001. Mary is my niece, and Dayne is her son. Mary is a special ed teacher near her home in Bogart, Georgia. One day she took some gifts to school to give to each of her kids (I think she has six or seven in her class). One little boy didn't open more than one of his gifts. She asked him about it and found out he wanted to take them home to share. He told her, "My mother is crying." She asked why, and he said there was no one to help her with Christmas this year.

Well, Mary got others to help her, and she gathered up a bunch of food and had her husband, Dexter, and a sister-in-law, Lisa, take the stuff over (the family would have recognized Mary). Dexter told Mary that the mother was so thankful she couldn't handle it. She said things like, "Oh, you cannot imagine how much we needed this!" Dexter said he had to pull Lisa off the porch because she was losing it big time. She had looked in the house at the rather small and bare tree, and there was just one little gift sitting on the floor. So Mary and the others went to work again, gathering and wrapping gifts and getting contributions. Mary was on the phone a lot. After one conversation, she hung up and noticed Dayne (who had just turned nine) looking at her intently. "What does *contribution* mean?" he wanted to know. "What's a contribution?" Mary explained about the little boy and the family that didn't have Christmas. She told him, "Look at all the wonderful gifts under our tree. They have only one gift under their tree. So we're going to help them."

A little while later, Dayne came and handed her about $2 and asked her if she could make sure the family got it so they could have a happy Christmas. It tipped her right over. She cried and hugged him. Later she was in straightening up his room and found his wallet, open and empty—he had given her all he had. Everything. She sobbed. She did again while she was telling me about it, and I cried too. It felt good to cry for something so sweet.

Later on, Dayne came to her with a pass-along card from the Church and asked if it would be okay to attach it to one of the presents. What a wonderful little man! Mary said when her co-worker went back to the home with a "ton" of wrapped gifts for everyone, the mother was overcome. "Who *are* you?" She wanted to know who they were, and why they were doing this, "What do you want from us?" Mary's friend responded, "*Nothing!* Have a very merry Christmas!" And the woman couldn't believe it. Just couldn't believe it.

Think about your own special stories of Christmas, or of any time of year. Have you written them down? Perhaps there are some experiences that need to be kept secret, but are there some that would be good to share in the family so they can be remembered as the years go by?

Last Lectures

I've been thinking about last lectures.

Several times I've heard of opportunities people have been given to present their "Last Lecture." They've been asked to choose a topic that would allow them to give their very last talk, the last message they would ever give, at least on this side of the veil. I've heard and read some of these talks, and I find them so interesting, so enriching, and so powerful.

You may remember the last talk Elder Bruce R. McConkie gave in general conference. It was Saturday morning, April 6, 1985. The title of his message was "The Purifying Power of Gethsemane," and it was a beautiful, tender, unforgettable testimony of the Savior. Listen to the way he began, and you get a sense that it will be his Last Lecture: "I feel, and the Spirit seems to accord, that the most important doctrine I can declare, and the most powerful testimony I can bear, is of the atoning sacrifice of the Lord Jesus Christ." And then just a part of his closing: " . . . I testify that [Jesus Christ] is the Son of the Living God and was crucified for the sins of the world. He is our Lord, our God, and our King. This I know of myself independent of any other person. I am one of his witnesses, and in a coming day I shall feel the nail marks in his hands and in his feet and shall wet his feet with my tears. But I shall not know any better then than I know now that he is God's Almighty Son, that he is our Savior and Redeemer, and that salvation comes in and through his atoning blood and in no other way" (*Ensign,* May 1985, 11). A few days later, on April 19, 1985, Elder McConkie went Home. His Last Lecture was one of his most powerful and beautiful.

When I'm reading the scriptures, particularly the Book of Mormon, I watch for these final words of the great prophets. After lives of incredible experiences and extraordinary service, what is it they want to tell us in their last few words? The first of the prophets named Nephi has several chapters that seem to constitute his Last Lecture. When you have a chance, read again chapters 25 through 33 of Second Nephi. For me it does make a difference to know it's a last message, a Last Lecture.

Moroni is one who has several Last Lectures. He doesn't know if he'll be around the next day, so there are a few times when he bids farewell. Beginning in Mormon 8, and for the next two chapters, he writes what might be termed a Last Lecture. But he lives longer, and is able to give us the book of Ether. He kind of interrupts himself in chapter 12 and gives another farewell before continuing with his account of what happened to Coriantumr and all the others. And, thankfully, we have the entire book of Moroni as well, including a powerful final testimony from Moroni inviting us to come unto Christ.

Joshua was about 110 years old when he shared this familiar message: "Choose you this day whom ye will serve; . . . but as for me and my house, we will serve the Lord" (Joshua 24:15). He died, leaving this as his last testimony (and invitation). Abinadi has a powerful farewell recorded, as does Samuel the Lamanite. Even some of the wicked people have interesting messages when it's time for them to leave, like Korihor (Alma 30:6–59) and Sherem (Jacob 7:1–23).

The Prophet Joseph Smith used an interesting phrase in Doctrine and Covenants 76:22–23 as he shared his and Sidney Rigdon's testimony: "And now, after the many testimonies which have been given of him, this is the testimony, last of all, which we give of him: That he lives! For we saw him, even on the right hand of God; and we heard the voice bearing record that he is the Only Begotten of the Father." The phrase "last of all" seems like an indication that this could be a fitting Last Lecture for the Prophet. Happily, he went on to write and say much, much more.

There are many more examples, but I want to also add that the Savior Himself gave some final instruction to His disciples. He asked them to "Go ye therefore, and teach all nations, baptizing them in the name of the Father, and of the Son, and of the Holy Ghost: Teaching them to observe all things whatsoever I have commanded you: and, lo, I am with you alway, even unto the end of the world. Amen" (Matthew 28:19–20). That's beautiful. He asked them to teach the gospel and then help people live it.

Have you ever thought about what you would include in your personal Last Lecture? I've tried doing this a few times, and it is a fascinating exercise. It takes my thoughts deep, deep down, way inside. How about giving it a try? It could certainly be in the form of a letter rather than a lecture. It could be addressed to anyone, to everyone, or to just one someone. Or even "To whom it may concern." What would you want to "say" at such a time?

So think with MEE. Think of what you'd like your family and other loved ones to know about how you feel about the most important things in your life. Think about it. This could be a wonderful soul search, a day of discovery, a time of deep and rewarding pondering.

First Things First

I've been thinking about putting and keeping first things first.

One day several years ago I was sitting on a plane looking at the phone snuggled into the back of the seat in front of me. There were little messages showing up, trying to entice me or my seatmates to use the phone. All you needed was a credit card and a willingness to pay a bill that would arrive eventually. At first I didn't pay much attention to what was happening with the phone because I knew I neither needed nor wanted to use it. But then, for some unknown reason, I began paying attention. I noticed the scrolled message that flashed on every once in a while, alternating with some instructions about how to insert your credit card. There were three suggestions: "*Check Voice Mail." "*Call the Office." "*Call the Kids." Interesting list of priorities, and an interesting order—first check your voice mail, then call your office, and then call your family.

I began thinking (again) about what I put and keep first in my own life. If I made a list of just three calls I wanted to make from an airplane, what (or who) would be on the list, and in what order? I've heard, as you have, the invitation to live each day as though it were your last. I'd like to change that a little bit just to say that it's important to live each day—to *really* live. We need to be awake and aware and do the best we can to put and keep first things first.

What's first in your life? Sometimes it's possible for us to at least guess what's first by thinking about what we do first every day. Or what we spend the most time doing. Or what we do when we're in our best mood. Or what we choose to do when there are many possibilities. When I was in college, we had to keep track of the food we ate for a week, probably for a nutrition class. We were supposed to write down everything. I think the motto of the class was, "You are what you eat." I was one big snack!

I'm thinking the same thing might work for the way I use my time. Maybe it would help to write down where it goes. Shall we try it? Let's not get *too* detailed, but just make a general list of where our time each day is spent.

Maybe we can then compare our list of where the minutes went with our list of what means the most to us in
our lives. You might have the same realization I did: that
much of my time (too much) is spent on things that "pop
up," and that aren't very high on my list.

My experience on the airplane with the "three calls
list" happened several years ago but has been on my mind
ever since. You would guess that I added a whole chunk
of additional thoughts after the events of September 11,
2001. I don't recall reading about people with cell phones
aboard the plane or trapped in the towers carrying on
much business that day. I didn't read about anyone calling
to check on the stock market or to say they might be late
to a meeting. They called their loved ones. They called
their families to express their love and to say good-bye.
Thousands of times, loved ones heard: "I love you."
"Mom, I love you." "First, I want to tell you guys I love
you." And they heard so many other things. "I need you
to be strong for me." "There's too much smoke." "I'm
still here in the office. I'm okay." "I love you; stay on the
line." "We're having problems, but I'm comfortable . . .
for now." "I know we're not going to make it out of
here." "I think we're going down, but don't worry. It's
going to be quick." "Are you ready? Okay. Let's roll."

What would you do if you were ever in such a circumstance? Who would receive a call from you if you had just three calls you could make, and you knew they'd be your last? What would you say? Maybe we can think about such things—about putting and keeping first things first, even on days when there aren't emergencies or tragedies. We can choose to call and tell someone we love them and that they matter to us—just because.

Road Rage

I've been thinking about road rage.

One day I realized that I frequently use driving as a way to describe my need to keep working *hard* on being a more Christlike, kind, gentle person. Someone came up to me after a recent talk and said, "You need a chauffeur!" Obviously I had once again spoken about my efforts to be a kinder, gentler driver.

When I'm driving in unkind ways (I'd appreciate it if you wouldn't ask me to explain or illustrate, please, just use your own experience or your imagination) like a no-heart racer, I'm positive no one is looking at me thinking, "That sure reminds me of Jesus . . . that reminds me of what the Savior would do." Probably just the opposite. They might be thinking someone was watching MEE when they came up with the term *road rage.* Oh, I hope not!

One of the many things I've learned about myself is

that when I'm in a hurry, the cars in front of me become an annoyance. When I want to just wander along, the cars behind me become the annoyance. Funny, isn't it? *I'm* never the one "at fault"; it's always either the ones in front or the ones behind. I'm perfect. I drive just the way I'm supposed to. I'm an excellent driver.

I've tried to teach myself some specific things I can do to be a better driver. And I'll pass some of them along in case they might be of some help. I am actually making progress! I'm getting better! (But it might be true that I do need a chauffeur.)

One thing I do that makes a big difference is to leave early for appointments. And I talk to myself. "You have plenty of time. You're not in a hurry. Relax." Things like that. I remind myself that I don't have to be anxious and competitive. When you're driving, if you feel competitive and angry at other drivers, let them win! What have they "won"? Position on the highway? Five seconds? And what have you lost? Pride? Anger? Say in your heart, "Your mother must be very proud of you!" You'll feel better about "losing." You'll feel less "rage."

In the past, I've loved the feeling of "winning"—beating another driver to an off-ramp or a light or something like that. Okay . . . I admit I still do that. But not as often. There's an even better feeling: letting someone in. Smiling and motioning someone to pull in front of you. Pulling into a parking place farther away, letting someone behind you pull in closer and think what a lucky day they're having.

Elder Neal A. Maxwell tied much of our behavior to selfishness in an address in general conference in April 1999. "Selfishness likewise causes us to be discourteous, disdainful, and self-centered while withholding from others needed goods, praise, and recognition as we selfishly pass them by and notice them not (see Morm. 8:39). Later on come rudeness, brusqueness, and the further flexing of elbows. In contrast to the path of selfishness, there is no room for road rage on the straight and narrow way" (*Ensign,* May 1999, 23).

President Hinckley spoke of anger as an addiction, and specifically mentioned road rage. "We hear much these days of the phenomenon called road rage. Drivers become provoked over some small irritation. They fly into a rage, even resulting in murder. A life of regret follows. . . . Let no member of this Church ever lose control of himself in such an unnecessary and vicious manner" (*Ensign,* May 1998, 50).

I've felt regret. Not that I've murdered anyone, but

there have been times when I've felt regret at being impatient and mad. Guess what I thought of when I was pondering all of this (one of the many times). I thought of the advice of counting to ten. How about that as one idea? By the time we count to ten (unless we cheat and do it by twos, or go too fast), we could think of something better than an angry reaction to what's going on around us. This is the kind of driver I'd like to be: I'd like it to be true that others were glad I was on the same road at the same time, because I could be counted on to be patient, kind, and helpful.

Maybe I'm not the only one struggling to be more patient, more civil. Is there anyone else out there who understands what I'm trying to say? I am a covenant person. One of my covenants is to be a witness of Christ at all times, in all places—even when I'm driving. When you see me next, pass me a note with some of your ideas for slowing down, being more patient, and increasing self-control, peace, and Christlike behavior. Let me know what you've been thinking. I know we can help each other. The Savior promised His disciples peace, and we can receive the same magnificent blessing as we work to overcome our selfishness, our pride, our impatience, and our lack of charity.

Resumés

I've been thinking about resumés.

Actually just one, for the most part: *my* resumé. Sometimes, when someone asks for your resumé, do you ever wish you could give them something that would knock their socks off? Often I include facts from my life that aren't usually known. Want some examples? (Skip this next part if your answer was "no.")

General of Recess War Games, East Elementary, two years

Cabin Maid, Zion National Park, the summer I was sixteen

Curio Shop Clerk, Zion National Park, the summer I was seventeen

Salesman, *Humpty Dumpty Magazine,* for quite a while

High-Jump Champion, sixth grade (I should have apologized to Kent; he cried)

First Prize, Easter Art Contest, fifth grade (for
which I received a record about "The
Churckendoose")

Contributor to "Newsette" (in the *Deseret News*),
and I still have my badge

Neighborhood Marble Champion (I've been told
I don't have all my marbles)

Violinist with four orchestras

Danced at Janet Jones's wedding (group, not solo)

I can even put on my resumé that I have performed
in the DeJong Concert Hall at BYU and Symphony
[Abravanel] Hall in Salt Lake City! I know you'd ask in
amazement if you could, so let me explain. I've had the
chance to speak a couple of times in the DeJong Concert
Hall, on a Sunday, and I sang opening and closing hymns
with those who came—so I have indeed "performed."
And Symphony Hall? Well, again, I had a chance to
speak there once, and it occurred to me that this was my
big chance, my one and only opportunity. So I explained
to the audience that I wanted to be able to say I'd performed there, and I proceeded to sing the first part of
"Born Free." Of course it could never even come close to
the time I was there in Symphony Hall with Carol to

hear Jesse Norman perform the last four songs of Strauss . . . but I did perform.

Now, all these things are true. You can list your own things—make your own resumé. But what about the things you wish you had done, things you've dreamed about? Okay! Now you're talking!

> Pirate (Sea name: Heave-Ho . . . I get motion sick!)
>
> Cowboy at a ranch in Montana (Ranch name: Sage Rage)
>
> Guide for Marco Polo expedition (Nickname: Fodor)
>
> Soprano or Tenor with the Metropolitan Opera (I like the name Carmen Ghia, however it might be spelled)
>
> Orchestra Conductor (Madame Tuneinforken) (Hitanei) (Tunemup)

Then I thought some more. After a *lot* of happy laughing—I haven't even begun to list all the things that came to my mind—I settled down a bit and decided these are things I'd love to have on my resumé:

Worked hard at doing good and being good.

Finally became like a child.

What about you? What would you like on your resumé? How about starting by listing things that could already be put there? List the things you enjoy doing, the things you're good at doing. Don't leave anything off just because it doesn't seem like it belongs on a resumé (just use another word if *resumé* is too much). Doing handwork, baking bread, listening, making cabinets, playing a harp, teaching. Don't you agree that there's a lot more to living than having one or two fancy things to include on a resumé?

I'm inviting you to think in two ways. One is to list things you already have done and know how to do (without trying to evaluate their importance in a somewhat topsy-turvy world). The other is to think of things you'd like to include some day—talents and accomplishments, yes, but also characteristics.

Another way to do this—a bit of a twist on the resumé idea—is to write a talk you'd like someone to give at your funeral. I almost didn't put that in here because it might seem morbid or insensitive. I just mean it as another way of asking yourself how you want to be remembered—what you want and hope to be. So think about it. Your resumé. Your "bio." Whatever you might call it. Enjoy!

Visual Aids

I've been thinking about visual aids.

I suppose in some sense you could say that glasses, contact lenses, binoculars, and a bunch of other things are "visual aids." But I'm thinking about the kind that illustrate lessons and presentations and such. For example, someone who is teaching a lesson about Noah might bring a collection of animals to class (two each). Not really *big* animals, but just some "samples." Something like that.

I want to set up a situation and have you think about what you'd do. This is taken from something that happened to me. I was serving a mission in Indonesia, and one of the things we did was to help people with ideas on becoming effective teachers. There wasn't much translated into the Indonesian language at the time, but we did have some materials in English. One of our wonderful branch members whom I'll call Ibu Subowo knew a few words of English and asked to borrow our materials. She had a great desire to become a better teacher in Relief Society. One day during her preparation and study time she came across the term *visual aids*. She didn't understand what it meant. She had an English-Bahasa dictionary, so she looked up the words. When she figured out what it meant, she made a plan and began working on her visual aids for her next Relief Society lesson.

In this place in Central Java where paper and pencils were both luxury items and not abundantly available, this dear soul wrote out her entire lesson on about eight pieces of paper. When it was time for her class, we noticed that Ibu Subowo had hung these pages on the wall of the part of the rented home that we used for our Relief Society meetings. We arrived a little bit early, and she came running to us to ask, "How do you like my visual aids?" Here's the part where I'd like to have you think with MEE. My question is: What do you say to Ibu Subowo? She has worked hard—no doubt about it. She is obviously excited about her first formal effort in making visual aids. It's just about time for class to begin. Again: What do you say? How do you respond to her?

What if we said to her, "Well, those look more like

your notes than visual aids." Or what if we started to laugh? Or what if you and I looked at each other and pulled some faces and shrugged, not knowing what to say? You can't stand any of those responses, can you? Your heart won't let you respond that way. You would say something positive, wouldn't you? "I can tell you've worked very hard to prepare your lesson and these visual aids. It's obvious you care very much about the sisters in your class." You'd say something like that. Not overly gushy—"Oh, these are the best and most fantastic visual aids I've ever seen in all my years as a person!" No. You're honest. Positive and honest. It just may be that Ibu Subowo will say something after the lesson.

And that's what actually happened. She said she noticed that most of the sisters in the class couldn't see what she'd written. She asked for ideas. You and I could suggest that maybe it would help for her to select some of the most important words, then make them bigger and put fewer on a page.

This incident with Ibu Subowo happened "long ago and far away," but it's something you do all the time. You're so good at this. Someone works hard on a project and you give honest praise. *You* are a "visual aid" for the way we ought to encourage and support each other.

Good for you! The world needs more compliments. Thanks for passing them around so freely and generously. Can you think of someone who needs a note, a phone call, a comment from you?

Zoramites

I've been thinking about Zoramites.

I was reading in the book of Alma (chapter 31) in the Book of Mormon one morning in the fall of 1997, thinking again about how awful those apostate Zoramites had become. Here comes this "crackerjack" missionary team of Alma Junior (fresh from his encounter with Korihor) and his companions: Ammon, Aaron, Omner, Amulek, Zeezrom, and two of Alma's sons, Shiblon and Corianton. Alma had received "tidings" (I've always connected that word to "glad tidings," but in this case they were anything but glad) that the Zoramites were "perverting the ways of the Lord." What Alma heard sickened his heart and caused him great sorrow. These were people who had been part of the Nephites but had separated themselves. And it hadn't taken very long for major changes to happen.

So Alma determined to go on a mission, hoping that

the preaching of the word would once again have a powerful effect upon minds and hearts. I admit that sometimes when I've read the chapter I've thought it would be good for Alma to call down plagues—floods, flies, famine, or some other disaster—to wake the Zoramites up and remind them of how far they'd strayed. When the missionary team arrived, they discovered that these dissenters had "fallen into great errors." Alma and his team were "astonished" at what they observed and learned. And this is where we hear about "Rameumptom," the place where they "prayed."

One early morning I was reading along, thinking how far those people had gone from the truth and from true worship in such a short time. How *could* they? What were they *thinking?* And then a very powerful, personal message came into my heart, almost like a shock. I wrote at the bottom of the page in my Book of Mormon: "How much am I like this—a 'one-day-a-week' member with memorized prayers, feeling separate, filled with pride, boasting in ways of which I'm unaware, setting my heart upon 'all manner of fine goods,' and puffed up with the vain things of the world?"

That idea caused me to do some soul searching, and I realized that perhaps the Zoramites hadn't "exploded" away from keeping their covenants and following true ways of worship. Maybe their apostasy involved more a collection of little things, like thinking their prayers would be more effective if they crafted the words and climbed on high places. Little things, like beginning to feel that they were holier and more favored ("elected") than others. I thought about having heard for much of my life about "where much is given," and the blessing of being born in the covenant to parents who taught me well, growing up in a free land, having enough and more of food and clothing and opportunities. Were these things that I allowed to make me feel separated from millions of others who hadn't had the same chances? Have I sometimes thanked God that I'm a "chosen and holy person," judging (even if without realizing it) all those who weren't "chosen and holy"?

And then in Alma 31:23 there was one more specific, in-my-heart message on an important morning: "Now, after the people had all offered up thanks after this manner, they returned to their homes, never speaking of their God again until they had assembled themselves together again to the holy stand, to offer up thanks after their manner." Wow. How often do I speak of and to God? Just once a week? Less? More? When was the last time I spoke of God to anyone? Has my communion to and about Him become diminished? Are my prayers pretty much "memorized" to the point where they're "routine" and without real feeling? I then read verse 25 again, looking for a key to what happened, and what grieved Alma so much. "Yea, and he also saw that their hearts were lifted up unto great boasting, in their pride." There followed a soul cry from Alma as he prepared for the task of giving his all to try to bring these souls back to Christ and the truth. "O Lord, wilt thou grant unto us that we may have success in bringing them again unto thee in Christ. Behold, O Lord, their souls are precious, and many of them are our brethren; therefore, give unto us, O Lord, power and wisdom that we may bring these, our brethren, again unto thee" (Alma 31:34–35).

And there was a cry in my own soul as I wondered how much I'd neglected in bringing my own soul back to Christ and to my Heavenly Father. I don't remember the exact morning when this particular chapter in Alma awakened me to my own lack of passion and excellence, but it was extremely helpful. Chapter 32 may be more "popular" and more often quoted, but for me on this morning of discovery I came to treasure Alma chapter 31 in a very personal, meaningful way.

Have any thoughts come to you as you've read this chapterette? Can you find, as I can, some ways in which drifting can happen—a gradual (or sudden) move toward Zoramitish behavior? Can we pull these weeds out of our souls before the roots go too deep?

Going Home

I've been thinking about going Home.

Notice that I put a capital *H* on the *Home* part. Death is a holy thing. It's the process of returning Home. I wish we weren't so frightened of this change, this transfer. I wish it weren't such a difficult thing to experience for those of us "left behind."

Alma Junior teaches comforting truth regarding this process to his son Corianton in the Book of Mormon: "Now, concerning the state of the soul between death and the resurrection—Behold, it has been made known unto me by an angel, that the spirits of all men, as soon as they are departed from this mortal body, yea, the spirits of all men, whether they be good or evil, are taken home to that God who gave them life. And then shall it come to pass, that the spirits of those who are righteous are received into a state of happiness, which is called paradise, a state of rest, a state of peace, where they shall rest

from all their troubles and from all care, and sorrow"
(Alma 40:11–12).

I've had some sweet experiences with death. One
comes to mind that happened while I was teaching nursing at BYU in the mid-1960s. I was working with students on Pediatrics. On this particular morning, I had
made an assignment for Gwen (not her real name) to
take care of Matthew (not his real name either). Everyone
knew the little fellow wouldn't live long following his
arrival to inhabit his tiny, misshapen, inadequate body. I
don't remember all that was wrong with him, but I clearly
remember the dimples where eyes should have been. And
I can still hear the kind of wail that would come from his
room when he was crying.

I felt that caring for this baby would be a tender, significant experience for Gwen. She arrived a little before
7:00 A.M., and I handed her the assignment. It had
Matthew's room number and a little bit about his condition. I was busy getting all the students started with their
morning routine when I noticed Gwen waiting to talk to
me. She was a rather quiet and timid student, and I
immediately felt concerned. She looked upset and was
fighting tears. "I can't do it . . . I just can't do it. Please
can you change my assignment?" I asked her to tell me

what had happened. She said she had gone to the room and had been shocked to see Matthew with all his physical problems. She said she felt overwhelmed and completely inadequate, even frightened.

Not wanting to add to her trauma, I did change her assignment. But later in the morning I asked if she would come with me to visit Matthew. She agreed. We went into Matthew's room, and it was just the three of us. I'd had a feeling that it might help her if I spoke for Matthew—got acquainted with her and let her get acquainted with him through me. I asked her some questions about herself: where she was from, why she had decided to be a nurse, what she liked most about it, and what she found the most challenging.

Then, as Matthew, I told her I knew she'd been shocked and upset when she first came in the room. "I know it's hard to look at me. I don't know what I look like, but I know I'm not like any baby you've ever seen. Can you imagine *my* shock at being assigned to this body? It seems like almost *nothing* looks or works the way it's meant to!" I went on, speaking for Matthew, praying that I wasn't doing anything too far over some line of appropriateness. My desire was to help Gwen see Matthew in an entirely different way—and I later wished

I had done that before giving her the assignment. Through me, Matthew asked her if she had any questions. I think she asked if there was much pain. I said not really, that most of my crying was because I felt lonely and frightened. I told her that "I get hungry like any baby does, and I like to be clean and dry. I also like to be touched and talked to." This went on for maybe half an hour, and then Gwen asked if she could help feed Matthew. Absolutely! By the end of the shift, Gwen felt a tenderness toward Matthew that was wonderful to see. She asked if she could be assigned to him the next day, and I happily agreed. I felt it would be good for both of them.

On the third day that Gwen was assigned to care for Matthew, I arrived about 6:30 A.M. and found his room empty. When I asked where he was, I was told he had expired about an hour before I got there. They had put his little body in another empty room until someone came to pick him up. When Gwen arrived, I walked her to Matthew's room to show her it was empty. She looked at me with the big question. I said, "Matthew's gone Home."

"What? He's gone home?"

"He's gone Home." Then I asked her to come with

me. We walked into the darkened, quiet room where Matthew's little body lay, peaceful at last. At first she didn't understand. "You mean he's ready to go home, and they're going to come and get him?" She said she'd never seen him so deeply asleep and looking so peaceful and still. I said again, with emotion, "No . . . he's gone *Home.*" And then she understood. He was free from his little prison. He had indeed gone Home—back to that Father who had given him life and would certainly have welcomed him tenderly. Gwen and I shed some tears together. Matthew had been an incredible teacher.

As you've read this, perhaps you've thought of your own experiences with death—with trying to understand, with asking why, with wondering where your loved one has gone, with trying to adjust. Can you feel that what Alma taught Corianton is true? Can you feel that the people who have left have gone Home to God, and that they are resting from all their troubles, and from all care and sorrow?

Rice Christians

'**I**'ve been thinking about Rice Christians.

I wrote about this in a book for my friend Linda Kimball a few years ago and want to include some of the same thoughts in here so you can think with MEE.

"Rice Christian" is an interesting thing to call someone. I heard it a lot while I lived and worked in Southeast Asia for several years. I know for many it was and is used to describe someone who may have joined a particular religious or other group hoping for rice or other material handouts. I think I never heard the term used in a positive way. It was as if the person so called had no strong connection to Jesus Christ, and that any "conversion" was a matter of the stomach, not the heart.

Have I ever been that hungry, that desperate, so that I could understand such a thing? Have you? Did we miss something when we used that term? Did we judge? Were we terribly wrong to hastily put so many thousands in that handy category? Was there something deeply symbolic in the need for rice? Was it seen as more than physical food to those who may have received it? Was there a hunger and craving for nourishment both spiritually and physically?

Because of the tenderness shown to me in the sharing of this most basic of gifts, this rice, I wish to be known as a Rice Christian. This describes a connection between me and the many unforgettable saints of various religions who have so generously shared from their often meager stores. This is something that came from their hearts to mine as an offering of love and friendship, connection and esteem. Almost always it was a sacrifice. I was aware of one family who skipped several meals in order to share some rice with us. I'm sure this happened on other occasions but was kept a secret.

I was very interested to learn that in some cultures rice is sent along with those who have died so that they'll have some to sustain them along their journey. But rice was never thrown at people who were "just married."

It was in 1962 that I had my first encounter with rice as the center of attention at every meal. Before that I had always liked rice in almost any form. But we didn't eat it very often. Mostly it was something we had instead of potatoes from time to time. Or it was part of what we got when we ordered "Chinese food." I especially enjoyed it as a "leftover," with cheese melted and stirred in. "Cheese rice" is what we called it. Very original, don't you know.

In Asia, and perhaps other places as well, rice was much more than a "side dish" or a substitute for anything else. It was the center of the meal, with all else supplementing and complementing the fluffy white heaps of *bigas* or *nasi* or whatever it might be called. For some families, rice seemed to be their "glue of the day." Rice in Asia wasn't a package, it was a process. It was the "Law of the Harvest" up close and personal. Even those who bought it in the market in huge baskets (priced according to how many rocks and other impurities were still left for removal at home) knew the process very, very well.

How many paintings on black velvet have I seen depicting people bending over to stick the little seedlings deep in the mud? I have watched people standing in the water planting the seedlings of rice. I've seen the extraordinary network of waterways on the sides of hills in Taiwan, the Philippines, Indonesia, and other places, with the beautiful, distinct green that indicated the tiny plants were beginning to grow in their water beds. I remember watching a man in Hong Kong carefully watering his small rice paddies with two watering cans balanced across his shoulders with a bamboo pole. I've observed the beautiful green fields turn to the ripened color of mature rice. I've had a chance to watch the harvesting process, again done by hand. And I've seen all the stacks of rice for sale in the open marketplace. I remember feeling like a little child as I waited for the "Puffed Rice Man" to come in Taiwan. We'd take our little bag of "raw" rice out to him, and he'd heat it up and shoot it out of a cannon, just like it says in some kind of advertising. Only it was a very simple, old-fashioned "cannon."

One experience that helped me understand the value of rice—of even one grain of rice—happened in a refugee camp in Thailand. During a visit to one makeshift shelter, I was enjoying watching some children playing in the small area in front of their place. One of them accidentally knocked a bag of rice over, and some of it spilled. I watched the family patiently pick up every grain of rice and put it back in the bag, and I thought of how many grains of rice I had wasted in my life. I knew this was an important lesson for me—something to think about.

I want you to think with MEE about that, about how much we waste of food, water, and other resources. Can we be more careful? In Indonesia my heart was touched deeply as I learned of the consecration of members of the local branch to which I belonged in Central Java. The Relief Society president, Ibu Subowo, had invited each member to save one spoonful of uncooked rice before beginning to prepare food in the morning. Each sister would bring her tiny plastic bag of rice to Relief Society, her holy contribution to be shared with someone in need. I wonder what the equivalent would be for me if I were to try to make such a donation. Rice wasn't cheap, as I had thought it would be, and the people in this part of Indonesia made an average of about $125 per year. My equivalent might feed a small country for a day or more!

Because of all the rice that has been so generously shared with me in a variety of circumstances, I have been blessed. I have memories connected with the fluffy white stuff—sometimes with rocks and other surprises, but always with love and friendship—that cannot be erased from my heart. For the most part, these memories are connected to unselfish brothers and sisters with kind, brown faces and dark, gentle eyes. Inasmuch as the rice was shared with MEE, one of the least of these, it was shared with the First Christian, the Savior (see Matthew 25:34–40).

I bless all those who have shared with me of their precious daily rice, and I join them in considering myself a Rice Christian. What about you? Has this chapterette brought any particular experience to your mind?

Courage

I've been thinking about courage.

This time I'm thinking about courage as it relates to trying new things. Think about your life. How often do you do something you've never done before? See, this is a chapterette where I want you to start thinking right at the beginning. "Prelude thinking." Do you find that you're doing more and more and more of less and less and less? (You might have to read that over a few times to catch on to what I mean . . . give it a little time.)

I'm trying to say that without courage, without daring to try new things, we may come to a point where our lives are narrowing, closing in on us. We have routines and patterns and habits that are almost smothering. We actually *are* doing more and more and more of less and less and less. We keep repeating the same things. We even get to a point where we sit in exactly the same place for meetings or classes or other events. We drive exactly the

same way to work or school or appointments. In the grocery store, we go up and down the same aisles in the same
way every time (maybe even buying the very same
things).

Now, recognizing that there are some things we
should *not* change, I'm going to offer a suggestion: Do
something every day that scares you half to death! Ha.
You have to think about that one a little bit, don't you?
I'm suggesting that we have the courage to try new
things, to change our routines often enough that we have
a fresh view of life, of our surroundings.

Once, when filling one's own car with gas was still a
new adventure, I decided it was time. I had known about
this "forever," but I still found comfort in pulling up to
the pumps where someone would do it for me. I've
always been afraid of the *unknown.* On this particular day
I decided to make myself brave and give it a try. I chose a
gas station where there weren't a lot of people around. I
don't know about you, but when I'm trying something
new, I don't want a whole lot of people hanging around
pointing and laughing. I won't go into details except to
say that I had gas down my leg and in my shoe before I
was finished. But I did it! I actually did it! And after that
first time I was anxious to try again, and I kept getting

better and better. Now I'm pretty good at it. I haven't filled my shoe for a long, long time.

I did something that scared me half to death (which, as always, is a bit of an exaggeration). So often that's so hard for me. To be honest, many of my scary things involve relationships—talking to others or doing things with or for others. I have great plans come into my head and heart, but I'm such a chicken when it comes to actually doing.

How about you? Are there times when you feel your life is getting rather narrow? Are there things you've thought you might enjoy, but you've been hesitant to try? It may be tennis or family history work. It could be a book club or sewing. It could be piano lessons or basic auto mechanics. It could be contacting a long-lost friend or smiling at others. Think about courage—about doing things you've never done before, or just things you want to do more often. And think about doing something every day (a *good* thing) that "scares you half to death." Try something new. See if some new doors and windows open for you.

The Best You Can Do

I've been thinking about doing the best you can do.

When I was first called on a mission in 1962, there was no language training before going to the field. Like everyone else, I had one week in the Missionary Home in Salt Lake City, and then off I went to Asia. My first assignment was to go to Taiwan. The language I was to learn was Mandarin. The other missionaries asked if I knew any Chinese, and I said, "Yes: Ah so." They said that was Japanese, so I started "in the hole."

Mandarin did *not* sound like a language to me. It sounded like little bursts of noise. I couldn't imagine that everyone didn't think this was hilarious—saying these little noises to each other! Each noise was the sound of a character. A one-syllable noise for each of the thousands of characters. *Plus,* each noise had a tone. Yes. Each specific character had a specific noise *and* a specific tone. To make words, characters were put together, and noises and tones. Wrong tones, wrong word. Sounds complicated. Was. I think most of us missionaries practiced doing the tones by moving our heads in different up-and-down motions to indicate which tone we hoped we were "hitting." Our companions were our teachers, and they could play some tricks. And did. Once I went in the post office and asked for twelve red monkeys.

Slowly but surely, though, I started to recognize a few words. I could say "good morning," "how are you," and the name of the Church (lots of head-bobbing on that one). After I had caught onto some basic things, my companion, Jan Bair, began to help me learn the Joseph Smith story. Each morning we'd ride our bikes to the edge of the city where we lived in the south of Taiwan, and she'd help me practice. It still didn't sound or feel like a language; I was just concentrating on noises and tones. One day she said, and I quote, "You're ready!"

To be honest, I didn't *want* to be ready. I didn't want to have to do my noises and tones "in public." It was hard to resist praying that no one would let us in that day. But someone did: Sister Lin. I was listening to the sounds, not understanding much of what was going on, and doing my part with the flannel board—yes, this "dates" me—when I got a signal from Sister Bair. Then things went really quiet. All eyes (four) were on me. It was time.

And now comes one of the best lessons I ever learned. In that moment, all I could do was the best I could do. Do you know what I'm saying? All I could do was the best I could do. And so, here they came, the noises and tones, with my head doing some kind of accompaniment. And guess what the Holy Ghost did. As those noises went out into the air, He took them over to Sister Lin, and as they entered her ears, her mind, and her heart, she learned that a young boy went into a grove of trees to pray and was visited by the Father and the Son. Imagine! Think of it! Really think of it!

I pass along that incredible moment to you and say with much feeling that what God asks of us is the best we can do. I'm convinced He knows that we have different kinds of moments and days and seasons, but He is never asking more than our best. I do admit that there are times when He will ask for more than we think we can do, but it isn't more than we can do *if* we'll let Him help us. Think of the wonder of that, and the comfort in it. He asks for the best we can do, and for what we can't do, He "fills in." We do what we can, and He does what we can't.

Exercise

I've been thinking about exercise.

Here is one of those things that I know is good for me. I know it! And sometimes I'll exercise for a day in a row (maybe two if the weather's nice and I'm in the mood), and then it's over. One brief moment, and I'm finished. "That was nice. I can do it anytime I want."

I can tell anyone that I exercise regularly, and they are so impressed. But I always hope they won't ask any probing questions, because they'd find out that I exercise once in April and then again in November. I've learned that there is nothing like sitting briskly for good exercise! Don't you love that?

Let's suppose the very thought of exercise brings on shallow breathing and a rash. I'm just saying that it might make us nervous—it might seem like a mountain that's way too high. How about if we just start where we are and do *something?* I think it makes a difference even if we just take a dozen or so deep breaths every morning.

Exercising really is so good for us. It's cheap health insurance. It increases our well-being both physically and mentally. Find something you enjoy doing (in case some of the ideas I share don't quite work for you) and stick with it. Actually, I go out for a walk in the early mornings. I like listening to the birdies as they holler at each other, talking about dreams and other adventures that happened during the night. Sometimes I go say hello to the three young buffalo that live near our stake center. I love to watch sunrises, and I've seen some amazingly beautiful ones. It's a time for me to ponder, to think about the coming day and days, to communicate with Heavenly Father about how beautiful everything is.

Think about the difference it can make if you find time for exercising—on a walk, in the living room, at a gym, at the mall or another place where they welcome walkers, on your treadmill or stationary bike (when I first heard that I thought maybe it was a bike that would write letters for you!), in your aerobics class, swimming, playing tennis, riding your bike, throwing javelins, hiking, jogging . . . find what you can fit in to your schedule, what is enjoyable, and away you go!

But I want to help more than that, so I have devised several exercises that I am convinced will make a big difference for all of us. I just wish I could share the illustrations that go with these particular exercises! Here's the first one: the Follicular Extension Exercise. Assume a kneeling position. Get comfortable. Now fold your arms across your chest. Keeping your head perfectly still, extend your hair vertically as far as possible. Hold. Release gradually. Relax. Repeat. Doesn't that feel good?

Now another one: the Tarsal Contusion Exercise. You might not want to do this one on your driveway or in your unfinished basement. Stand erect with arms held firmly at your sides. Keeping your muscles rigid, lean forward on your toes and fall flat on the floor. Relax and repeat. If necessary, you might ask someone to bind your wrists with a leather thong to keep you from cheating. This is an amazing exercise!

And the last one in this series is the Lingual Distension/Extension Exercise. Lie face down on the floor with your hands clasped firmly behind your head. Keeping your muscles rigid, extend your tongue and raise your body from the floor in a push-up motion. Lower slowly. Relax and repeat. Don't you feel wonderful!? As you recover from these three incredible exercises, just think about how *good* you feel. Ha ha ha.

Comfort Zones

I've been thinking about comfort zones.

"Leaving our comfort zone" has come to mean doing things that are hard to do, that are uncomfortable, that stretch us and help us grow. Well, I've been thinking about this in a different way. I'm feeling that sometimes we need to come *back* to our comfort zone. Can you imagine what I mean by that? I mean that there are times when we feel so very uncomfortable because we're where we shouldn't be, not just in terms of a place, but in terms of who we are and what we're doing. And what we're becoming.

Maybe we've let go of the iron rod. Maybe we've reached a point where to some degree we're both *in* the world and *of* the world. Maybe we've slipped into some habits that are feeling destructive and foreign. There are times when we need to turn around and return to our comfort zone. We need to find a way to come back where we belong, and where we're safe.

The Savior is the ultimate source of this comfort and peace, this safe place for us to be. His arms are always reaching out to welcome us back to the fold. Yes, I believe in stretching (I hope you can tell that from other things you've read and thought about with me in this little book), and in meeting new opportunities and challenges with courage and enthusiasm, but I also believe we may sometimes stray too far from our Center and thus lose our sense of direction, purpose, worth, and connection to Holiness.

Think of where you are right now. Is it close to where you want to be? Is it far away? Would it feel good to come back to your comfort zone? Come on back. We'll watch for you. We'll wait for you.

Contention

I've been thinking about contention.

I tend to spend a lot of time thinking about things I'm working on. Contention is one of them. I want to get rid of it. Is this one you're working on too? Have you made some progress?

How I wish we could be sitting in a little group right now, sharing the adventures we've had as we've tried to become less inclined to stir up strife, to become angry, to quarrel and fight. Contention requires a winner and a loser—be sure to notice that the next time you're observing (or participating in) a contentious situation.

How about some "story problems"? I'll share some, and you may think up some others that would be even better and more relevant to your own circumstances and daily challenges. I'll share several, hopefully enough to really get you thinking.

You probably remember "story problems" from

school—the ones about trains leaving a station going x miles an hour and all that. You read the "story" or example, and then you figure out answers to puzzling questions. These twelve story problems won't be quite the same. They're not going to be about trains or boats or speed or distance or anything. They're going to be about us—about people, and about relationships. And about contention. As you read each one, think of what your first or "natural" reaction might be. Try thinking about what your reaction might be at different times of day or during different seasons (of your life and of the weather). Here we go!

1. A telemarketer calls and will not hear you saying "*No,* thank you."

2. Your neighbor has a son who has formed a little rock band (mostly drums), which practices in the garage right next to your bedroom. They begin their practicing between 9:30 and 10:00 P.M.

3. You're on vacation, in a line for the drive-up window at the bank, the kids are in the car, you've waited while four cars ahead of you have all been helped, and now, *finally,* it's your turn. You're a long ways from home. All you need is change for a $50 bill. You get to the

window, and they ask you if you have an account at that bank. You don't, so they refuse to give you change.

4. You're in a hotel, and the family staying above you has three children who are practicing for the vault for the Olympics, and because they're making a *lot* of noise, the parents have had to turn the TV up to an over-the-top volume.

5. You're on your way to an important appointment, and you left too late, and everything seems to go wrong. It's as if there are evil spirits working the traffic lights! You get almost to the intersection and BOOM, the light changes! And then you're in an area where you can't pass, and the car ahead of you is going below the speed limit, and the person driving it is glued to a cell phone.

6. You're at the grocery store, and all you need is some batteries for your hearing aid, and you're in a hurry, and you get in the "10 items or less" line with only one person ahead of you. And then you realize she has 57 items in her basket, and coupons for most of them.

7. You've been asked to speak in sacrament meeting and to take fifteen minutes. You've worked for two weeks and feel prepared with a meaningful message. The speaker ahead of you goes until about three minutes before the meeting is supposed to end.

8. You're the twelfth person in line at the post office, and there is only one person working at the counter. You get close and realize that the person three ahead of you has to get 47 money orders.

9. The repairman for your washing machine was due at 9:00 this morning; it's now almost noon, and he still hasn't come.

10. You're teaching a lesson at church, you've worked *so hard* to prepare, and there is someone in the class who can *not* allow you to get anywhere. They want to take over . . . and they *do!*

11. You're living in a small apartment near campus with five roommates and one bathroom. Enough said?

12. You're at an important conference, you *know* people aren't supposed to save seats, it's three minutes before the lecture is to begin, the ushers are indicating that the session is full, this is the class you *really* wanted to attend, and there's someone saving eleven seats right in front.

Have you had experiences anything like these? Was it hard not to feel "fighting mad"? How did you handle it? How *do* you handle it when you feel yourself boiling over? What I want us to think about (and this is where it would be great to have two or three or more gathered for a discussion) is how we could respond differently. What are some strategies for *not* reacting with anger? Does it help to count, literally, to ten? Does it help to put some humor in a situation? Does it help to pray instantly and earnestly?

There are probably some reading this who wonder what I'm talking about, who would naturally respond sweetly and gently to all of the above situations. In that case, I want you to think about how you can help the rest of us, okay?

Showing How

I've been thinking about showing how.

Maybe I can get you thinking if I tell you the opposite of showing how. It's showing off. Can you think of a time in your life when you had a chance to choose one or the other—when you could either show off or show how? Perhaps you were in a situation where it would have been so easy and so much fun to say to someone, "Well, I'm thinking of the time when I was serving as Relief Society president for the fourth time." Or, "That's something I learned how to do when I was seven years old." I think you're adding a few of your own now; that's good.

I've been working on having a show-how rather than a show-off heart. Let me tell you about a friend of mine who was a stake president with a show-how heart. One day he made a phone call to a man in the stake who had a son who was ready to be ordained an elder, and he wanted to find out what date would work for the father to perform that ordination for his son. The father seemed rather nervous about it and asked the stake president if *he* could do it. "Would you ordain my son for me?"

The stake president said he almost agreed, but then had a feeling. So he told the man he was coming over to visit with him for a few minutes. As they talked, the father admitted that he didn't know how. "I've never done anything like that. Please will you help me and ordain my son for me?" Another chance for the stake president, a wonderful soul, to say, "Sure—I'd be happy to help you. No problem." But, as I said, he had a show-how heart. He told the father he would show him how. They spent some time talking and practicing; then they set a date for the ordination.

On the Sunday morning when the ordination was to take place, the father came early and alone. He was so nervous he was shaking. "I can't do it. I just can't do it. I forgot every single thing you told me and every single thing we practiced. *Please* will you help me, President, and ordain my son?" Still another chance for a good stake president to step in and "help." But this wasn't just a good stake president—this was a *great* stake president. Oh, and did I mention he had a show-how heart?

"I'll tell you what we're going to do," he said to the

nervous father. "I'm going to stand right beside you, and I'll whisper instructions in your ear. I'll tell you everything you need to say and do."

The father wasn't sure this was "legal." "Can you do that?" he asked.

"Of course, because we're just about to do it!" And they did. This shy, loving father was able to ordain his son an elder with the help of a wonderful stake president.

When the stake president told me that story, he let me read a letter he'd received from this young elder while he was on his mission. He told of the marvelous experiences he was having, but then told the stake president that the greatest day in his life was the day when his dad ordained him an elder. He thanked the president for talking his dad into it—with the help of the Lord.

Now I think you can see what I mean, the difference between showing how and showing off. Think about situations where you can show how—with your children or grandchildren, maybe, or with nieces or nephews or neighbors. When you have a choice, see if it feels better to show how.

Investing in People

I've been thinking about investing in people.

I'm not sure you know anyone who'd fit in a "portfolio" (whatever that is), but I've just been doing a lot of thinking about helping people to help themselves and each other. I can remember asking missionaries how they thought it would make them feel when they had finished serving in a particular branch or area to have people say, as they were leaving, "We don't know what we'll do without you."

To tell you the truth, I think some of the missionaries thought that would be a sign of great love and affection. And I need to say that a comment like that probably *is* an indication of a sweet, memorable relationship. However . . . what if it's a literal thing? What if any of us were to go into a situation and become indispensable? Back to missionaries (of *any* age) as an example. What if a missionary were to write home something like this: "Oh, how the people need me! I don't know how they got along before I came, and I really don't know how they'll get along without me once I'm gone. I lead the singing (and sometimes I have to both lead *and* play), give talks, teach lessons, organize activities, do family home evenings for everyone, and on and on. I'm working so hard! I really think I'm making a difference."

As you think about it, do you notice anything wrong with this picture? The more I've thought about it, the more I've come to the conclusion that hearing "We don't know what we'll do without you" is *not* a compliment. It's not a compliment when a missionary hears this from members of a branch. It's not a compliment when a parent hears this from a child. It's not a compliment when a boss hears this from an employee. It's not a compliment when a teacher hears this from a student. Why not? Because I think we're supposed to be lifting, blessing, and enriching each other. I think we're supposed to be helping others to help themselves and each other. I think in so *many* of our relationships (not all!), we're supposed to be devoted to working ourselves out of a job. I think when we leave a person or situation, they ought to be better off than they were before we came.

I realized one day that I'd taught this concept often

when a teacher who had worked in my area at the MTC came to say good-bye. We had a good visit, and then when he got up to leave, he said, "I can go now. I don't need you anymore." We cried and hugged each other. I knew exactly what he meant.

I used to ask the missionaries to see if they could handle a compliment like *this:* "Thank you for coming. Look at all *we* can do because *you* came. You can go home now—we don't need you anymore." It's kind of like leaving yourself behind.

Imagine going back to where you served as a missionary, or running across someone you taught in a class, or, best of all, watching your children as they grow and move out and move on. Wouldn't it be great if you could see that in some ways you're still there? You have helped others to learn to fish (that great analogy), and now they are not only able to fish themselves but are teaching others to fish. You're carrying on! Think about your investments, and see if there are ways you can do more meaningful investing in people. Enjoy!

Titles

I've been thinking about titles.

I love to come up with titles. There's no way I could ever use them all, but I love thinking about them, seeing how many I can find as I put words together. Sometimes I like to think about variations on popular titles of things, and then go off on a long road of what I would include in an article or a book with a kind of "fractured title." Like "The Five Habits of People Who Aren't Very Effective." I could have such a good time with that one! Wouldn't we have fun if we worked on it together? Five habits such as being late, procrastinating, goofing off, cheating, sleeping through meetings, and being obnoxious. Oops—that's six!

One title I really love is "The Chicken Whisperer." That makes me laugh right out loud. I've told a few people I'm working on a book with that title. Even without ever doing it, it provides me lots of fun. How to talk a chicken into calmness and obedience. How to discuss the "crossing the road issue" with a chicken. How to get a wild chicken out on the range to leave its flock and come to you. Couldn't we have fun thinking about that?

How about "Men Are from Panguitch, Women Are from Manila." "Fodor's Guide to Kanarraville." "A Tree Grows in Beaver." "Dude the Obscure." And you don't have to stick just with book titles. Songs can be fun as well. "By the Time I Get to Elko." "Happy Trials to You." "I Did It His Way." And movies, like "Lassie Go Home." "One Flew over the Wasp's (or Squirrel's) Nest." "Magnificent Obstetrician." "Dances with Elves." (We could sell cookies!)

It's probably cheating to borrow and mess around with someone else's titles. But for me it's a fun place to send my mind for a little break. Think about some of the circumstances of your life, and see if you can come up with at least one title that fits. Give a title to one of your frustrating days. Give a title to a vacation you took that didn't turn out quite the way you had dreamed. Think of a title for a class you attended that you almost didn't survive, or a relationship that went "south."

Another thing you can do with titles (which might be more "dignified") is to think of writing the story of your life, and come up with titles for the different chapters or years or experiences. Okay, this little section didn't add much to your uplifting thinking, did it. But I hope it was fun. Think with MEE—see if you can just take a break by thinking of nonsense for a few minutes! Relax!

The Awards Assembly

've been thinking about awards assemblies.

We used to have these when I was in school. We would gather in the auditorium, and lots of parents and friends would come, and the school officials would be up on the stage, and names would be called for those who had won an award. Most popular. Best in math, music, art, sports. Most likely to succeed in business or friendship. Marble champion. You can think of more. I can feel it.

Pretend there's going to be an awards assembly in the Hereafter. Think of the clapping for the one who invented Velcro, Post-It Notes, chocolate, remote controls, ballpoint pens, Pentium chips, penicillin, zippers, paper clips, and so on. And how about the cheering for those who thought of and created things like the piano, jet engines, cement, submarines, the printing press, electricity, and gum. How exciting would it be to grant awards to amazing, courageous people like Martin Luther, Handel, Florence Nightingale, William Tyndale, Helen Keller, Columbus, Abraham Lincoln, Mother Teresa, Sir Thomas More, Joan of Arc, Gandhi, Thomas Jefferson, Beethoven, Bach, Victor Hugo, Leo Tolstoy, Jacques-Yves Cousteau, John Adams, and a whole bunch of others. And oh, the feeling as awards are given to Eve and Adam, Sarah and Abraham, Mary and Joseph, Emma and Joseph, and other great souls. And how about the joy of recognizing the work done by those who wrote the Bible and the Book of Mormon (including Mormon for condensing all those records, and Moroni for finishing it up so well and getting it safely buried).

Obviously they cannot all be listed—but think about it! What and whom would you add to the list? Add your own nominations for those to be honored at *the* Awards Assembly. And then an award (could it really be called that?) for the One who created the earth, flowers, birds, hope, sunsets, the Great Plan of Happiness, and *agency* . . . I think we wouldn't feel like clapping at that point. I think we wouldn't be able to do anything but *feel*. What do you think we'd be feeling? We'd probably just feel like shouting "Hallelujah!" and singing praises and expressing our joy and thanks!

Neighbors

I've been thinking about neighbors.

Several years ago I was scanning through the newspaper and noticed a small article with an intriguing title: "Unnoticed death brings soul-searching." I read the article and could hardly believe the story. In a community in central Massachusetts, it was discovered that a woman had been lying dead in her kitchen for four years! A little more than four years earlier, neighbors who hadn't seen her in a while inquired about her, but one of her brothers told police she had gone into a nursing home.

Since a formal missing-person report was never filed, there was no full-scale investigation. The police eventually found the decomposed body lying in a six-foot heap of trash she had let accumulate in her kitchen before her death. They believe she died of natural causes, but they found a telephone on the floor nearby, as though the seventy-three-year-old woman had tried to call for help.

The woman had been reclusive, and those in the neighborhood had tried to help her out by mowing the lawn and collecting her mail up until the time they thought she had gone into a nursing home. As one resident said, "People have their own lives. They go their own ways. They don't want to get involved. . . . Neighbors aren't like they were 20 years ago" (*Provo Daily Herald*, October 27, 1993).

Who is my neighbor? And how is my neighbor?

I grew up in the most wonderful neighborhood. Everyone was "Uncle" and "Aunt," even if we weren't actually related. I live in another wonderful neighborhood now. I remember street and block parties that offered everyone the chance to get better acquainted. During one of our parties we even showed slides (which we borrowed from everyone) on the side of our barn! Who is my neighbor? My neighbor is someone who needs me, and someone whom I also need.

I think the words *neighbor* and *neighborhood* are beautiful words. After thirty years of wonderful programs, Mr. Rogers finally hung up his sweater and put away his shoes, but will we ever forget, "Won't you be my neighbor?" and "It's a beautiful day in the neighborhood"?

Wouldn't it be an interesting thing to do with your

children: having them learn and then tell about the people in their neighborhood? One family had a special activity for a family home evening. They took their children for a walk around the neighborhood and talked to them about their wonderful neighbors. "On our way, we stopped in front of each house and told what we liked about the family who lives there." They talked to their children about the importance of being good neighbors also (Anita Thompson, "A Walk through the Neighborhood," *Ensign,* July 1987, 49).

I have to say here that if some of you reading this were to walk around your neighborhood, it might take you a couple of months.

Speaking to about 250 NAACP leaders several years ago, President Gordon B. Hinckley said: "In the course of my life I have mingled widely with people of all races, with those of Asia and Africa, Europe and Polynesia, with people in high station and low station, both good and bad. The world is my neighborhood, and its peoples, regardless of status, are my friends and neighbors. I include all within the compass of the mandate of the Savior, who said: 'Thou shalt love the Lord thy God with all thy heart, and with all thy soul, and with all thy mind. This is the first and great commandment. And the second is like unto it, Thou shalt love thy neighbour as thyself' (Matt. 22:37–39)" (*Ensign,* July 1998, 74).

We are to love God and our neighbor. We have neighbors across the seas as well as across the street. And sometimes a neighbor might be right in the same room. There shall be a gathering someday, a gathering of neighbors whose names we're not sure how to pronounce and whose villages we've never heard of.

Who is your neighbor? I invite you to walk or drive around your neighborhood, either literally or just in your mind, and remind yourself of who lives where, and how they're doing. Let's see if we can think of ways to promote a feeling of neighborhood as much as possible.